J. D Hayes

The Niagara Ship Canal

J. D Hayes

The Niagara Ship Canal

ISBN/EAN: 9783337127589

Printed in Europe, USA, Canada, Australia, Japan

Cover: Foto ©Andreas Hilbeck / pixelio.de

More available books at **www.hansebooks.com**

"THE NIAGARA SHIP CANAL:"

AND

"RECIPROCITY:"

PAPERS WRITTEN FOR THE "BUFFALO COMMERCIAL ADVERTISER,"

By J. D. HAYES, Esq.

TOGETHER WITH THE

SPEECH OF HON. ISRAEL T. HATCH,

IN THE CONVENTION AT DETROIT, JULY 14, 1865.

Published by Resolution of the Board of Trade, Buffalo.

BUFFALO:
PRINTING HOUSE OF MATTHEWS & WARREN,
Office of the Buffalo Commercial Advertiser.
1865.

THE NIAGARA SHIP CANAL SCHEME.

I.

The Niagara Ship Canal scheme having been before the public so long a time, and been considered of so much importance as to have engaged the attention of the various Boards of Trade throughout the country, many of whom have passed resolutions in its favor, and urged them with so much eloquence upon the attention of Congress as to secure the passage of a bill in one house appropriating $6,000,000 for the construction of the canal, there can be no impropriety in discussing the question of its necessity, even by so humble an individual as the writer of this paper.

All schemes for public improvement are proper for public discussion, and until the measures have become fixed laws, it is the part of wisdom to draw out facts and figures bearing upon the questions, if for no other purpose than to remove all doubts and hasten their construction in the shortest possible time, if they are real public necessities. If they are only selfish or visionary schemes, the sooner the public become acquainted with the truth, the better for all parties.

In treating this subject I propose to consider the general need of another ship canal around the Falls of Niagara as a Commercial, Political and Military necessity.

Commerce, like water, finds its own level, and is regulated by the law of supply and demand, except in a few cases of speculative movements, when the ordinary laws of trade seem to be lost sight of for the time being; and then the never-failing laws of supply and demand soon regulate the spasmodic effort, and apply the proper remedy.

Commerce must have its general commercial centre, and every country has its own commercial centre, from which the people get their commercial values, and make their exchanges, and to which the surplus productions of their staples are sent to market. The people of the United States recognize New York as our great commercial centre; and although Boston, Philadelphia, Baltimore, New Orleans, Cincinnati, St. Louis and Chicago are centres for local values, yet it will not be denied that New York is the great controlling centre of our commercial values and the place of shipment for our surplus productions. Admitting this fact, and then admit that the Great West is the chief grain-producing basin of the world, and it becomes a "commercial necessity" to transport the surplus productions of the West to the East by the most direct, safe and cheapest route possible.

In order to obtain these desirable ends, several leading men of Oswego, Detroit, Milwaukee, Chicago and other places have urged "The immediate construction of a ship canal around the Falls of Niagara by the general government, as a measure demanded alike by the interests of the producers West and the consumers East," and as a "military necessity."

Do the people of the United States desire to build this canal of such proportions as Congress proposes in its bill, merely for the purpose of getting from Lake Erie into Lake Ontario to facilitate the reaching of Boston or New York by that route? If so, what will be gained, unless you run down the St. Lawrence canals, out of the gulf, into the ocean and along the dangerous, rock-bound coast of Nova Scotia to those places? That is absurd, and is not worthy of a moment's notice. Therefore, when once into Lake Ontario, grain must be transferred at Oswego, and *from there it comes back again to the Erie Canal at Syracuse,* and reaches the same channel that it would by way of Buffalo without going into Lake Ontario at all. There is no other outlet, of any amount, for grain, unless the idea of a New York gentleman is adopted: to build a marine railway to take vessel and cargo by land into New York or Boston! This brilliant idea will be appreciated when the freight is paid on ship and cargo both instead of upon the cargo only. Here would be a good opening for investing the *surplus* funds of those gentlemen who propose to pay the national debt by subscription!

Unless it is desirable to change our commercial centre from New York to Liverpool, Montreal or Quebec, and to make use of the St. Lawrence canals for that purpose, what will be gained by transferring cargoes from Lake Erie into Lake Ontario? True, the canal tolls are less, and the canal shorter from Oswego than from Buffalo; but to off-set that it must be remembered that tolls on the ship canal and increased freight on the lakes will more than cover the difference.

It is urged that we must have increased facilities; that the increased productions cannot be moved without it. Let us examine the canal and lake facilities we now have, and see how much more we want — commencing at Buffalo:

Buffalo harbor is capable of accommodating all the vessels likely to go there for many years. It has a capacity for elevating from vessels into canal boats, or into store, 2,808,000 bushels of grain per day, and a storage capacity of 5,885,000 bushels. Suppose canal navigation to commence the 1st of May, and to close the 1st of December in each year, we have 184 working days. When worked to the full capacity, Buffalo alone could transfer from vessels into boats, or into store, 516,672,000 bushels. The most ever received in one year was in 1862, 58,642,344 bushels, leaving a capacity yet unoccupied of over 458,000,000 bushels, showing that only about one-tenth of the capacity has ever been used.

Complaint is made of the canals of the State of New York; that they are too small to furnish an outlet for Western shipments. Let us see how that account stands : The corrected register of canal boats now in the hands of the Collector at Buffalo, shows at the present time about 5,160 boats. The returns show, that for the local use of the State of New York eleven per cent. of the whole is required; deducting that from the total, leaves 4,592 boats for the through business; allowing thirty days for each trip, and each boat to make seven trips during the season, we have a total of 32,144 trips; allowing each boat to average only 6,000 bushels of all kinds of grain, and there is proved a *grain* capacity of 192,864,000 bushels. Deduct for the most ever shipped in one season, 58,642,344 bushels. and it shows a *grain* capacity left unused of over 154,000,000 bushels!

But it may be said that it is unfair to take all the capacity for grain, leaving nothing for such freight as lumber, staves, flour, provisions, etc. Let us see how the year 1864 stands upon the eastward bound through tonnage. These 4,592 boats, making 32,144 trips, their average tonnage being 141 tons each, give 4,532,304 tons capacity. The total through tonnage for 1864 was 1,907,136 tons, leaving a balance unoccupied of 2,625,168 tons, showing only about one-third of the tonnage used. The capacity of the boats now running is far below the average of what the canal can accommodate.

Many of the boats are of the old small class, while the canal is able to float a much larger class of boats. Those lately built and now building for the through business run from 200 to 250 tons. The boat Libby cleared from Buffalo, June 15th, 1865, with 7,850 bushels of wheat; others have cleared from Buffalo this spring with 8,300 bushels of corn. The boats D. C. Weed, E. C. Storck, John Austin and many others register 250 tons each, and the Francis Kenan, of Utica, registers 300 tons. It requires no more time or trouble to lock through a boat of 250 tons than one of 50 tons, when the locks are enlarged to admit them into the locks readily. Thus we may fairly claim that the capacity of the canal for through business (with the enlarged locks as proposed) will be equal to 6,000 boats of 220 tons each. These would move 1,320,000 tons each trip, and for the season of canal navigation could move 9,240,000 tons. The total through business of 1864 was but a trifle over one-fifth of the canal facilities with the enlarged locks. There may be a few days in the fall of the year, when the canal appears to be over-taxed, but if any one is able to build boats to run for those few days — and let them lay idle for the balance of the season — no one is disposed to hinder him.

Then what need is there for another ship canal at present? Are the rates too high? The canal is open to the whole world without regard to nationality or even color, to build and run just as many boats as they like, at just what price they like, over the State tolls; or three-fourths of the boats can be bought for less than their estimated value. The commercial law of supply and demand regulates the rates of freight, which are sometimes ruinously low, and at other times pay a fair profit. The average is not as profitable as in almost any other business where an equal amount of capital is at stake. Has the State been unfair in its dealings, and *increased* the tolls, that western men should seek to avoid them and take another route? Let us resort to figures again, both upon tolls and freight, taking the article of flour and tracing it through the various periods since shipments began to the present time, dealing with the general average for equal periods of years, for we must treat every great commercial business upon the *average* in order to arrive at correct deductions. We find that from 1830 to 1833 — four years — the toll on a barrel of flour, from Buffalo to Albany, was 51 cents, and the freight was 44 cents; the next twelve years the toll was 33 cents and freight was 42 cents, 40 cents and 27 cents for periods of four years each; the next four years tolls were 31 cents and freight 33 cents; the next, 25 cents tolls and 29 cents freight; the next, 23 cents tolls and 20 cents freight; the next seven years the toll was 19 cents and the freight 24 cents.

For thirty-five years western productions have been increasing at a rate never before equalled in any country, and during that time the tolls have been reduced sixty-three per cent., and the freight reduced forty-five per cent. on flour.

The State Auditor, Mr. Benton, says;

" Our rates of toll are not fixed upon a sliding scale, to rise and fall with the price of gold in New York, or the price of wheat and corn at Chicago, Buffalo, New York, or in London. In this fact the western producer has secured an important advantage."

The merchants also complain of the injustice done them; let us see how far the State is to blame in this matter. The averages on goods per 100 lbs. from Albany to Buffalo were as follows, viz.: First four years tolls were 49 cents and freight 45 cents; the next twelve years tolls were 33 cents and freight 57 cents, 45 cents and 26 cents, for four years each; next four years tolls were 24 cents, freight 15 cents; the next, tolls 19 cents, freight 11 cents; the next, tolls 15 cents, freight 10 cents; and the last seven years the average was 6 cents tolls and 6 cents freight. Thirty-five years of unexampled increase of the wealth and growth of our western towns and cities, and a decrease in tolls and freight the most remarkable ever known in the history of the world — the reductions being from 49 cents to 6 cents per 100 lbs. on tolls, and from 45 cents to 6 cents on freight, equal to eighty-eight per cent. in tolls and eighty-seven per cent. on freight; the extreme high price being paid cheerfully when we were *poor*, the low price now being a cause of complaint when we are rich and prosperous! This wonderful reduction in rates is a convincing proof that the vast and astonishing *increase* of population and production has been more than anticipated, until the increased facilities have far outstripped the demand, leaving hundreds of our canal boats lying idle during the greater part of the season, that would be useless entirely were it not for an increase of business during a few days in the fall. Those now running are scarcely paying expenses. Prices have fluctuated, and combinations have been formed to put prices up, and in some cases a few may have suffered by being caught in the gap; but competition is the great leveler of prices, and soon overcomes these irregularities.

To guard against combinations is one end to be gained, but this ship canal would not gain that end. The experiment has been tried for several years. The Welland canal has been open, and has been used for the very same purpose; and to show how perfectly commerce regulates itself it is only necessary to make a comparison of the average for the transportation of wheat and corn from Chicago to New York. For the year 1864, via lake and canal, via Buffalo, it was $28\frac{36}{100}$ cents on wheat, and $25\frac{49}{100}$ cents on corn; and via Oswego it was $28\frac{46}{100}$ cents on wheat, and $25\frac{90}{100}$ on corn. Saving in favor of Buffalo only one-tenth of a cent on wheat, and four-tenths on corn. Notice how evenly the charges are balanced in proportion to the work done by each route. The divisions of the charges by both routes for the average for the year were:

VIA BUFFALO.

Lakes Freight,	9 58-100	on wheat,	8 94-100	on corn.
Canal Tolls,	6 21-100	" "	4 83-100	" "
Canal and River,	12 57-100	" "	11 72-100	" "

VIA OSWEGO.

Lakes Freight,	15 37-100	on wheat,	14 28-100	on corn.
Canal Tolls,	3 54-100	" "	2¾	" "
Canal and River,	9 45-100	" "	8 87-100	" "

Thus while the charges on the totals were so nearly even, the State loses $2\frac{67}{100}$ on wheat, and $2\frac{89}{100}$ on corn, via *Oswego;* the difference of tolls and canal transportation being paid to the Welland canal, a foreign interest — and to the lake shipping, a purely local interest. The lake interest, in view of the dull summer season, desires this ship canal to occupy their vessels longer on the voyage, taking to themselves the difference in the tolls and canal rates, — one of the strongest reasons why every one having any interest in the State, particularly those having canal stock, should go against it.

The fluctuation in prices at times does not prove any fault in either route. It is an evil that cannot be controlled by State authorities or by the canal interests, neither is it confined to the canal. Take the last four years and see the fluctuations on the lakes and canals: the lowest average rate from Chicago to Buffalo, in 1861, was in July, when it was 5¾ cents on wheat, and 5¼ cents on corn. The highest was in October, the average for that month being $18\frac{36}{100}$ cents on wheat, and 17¼ cents on corn, — making a difference of about 350 per cent. between the months of July and October. On the canal from Buffalo to New York, the average for July was 11½ cents on wheat, and $10\frac{56}{100}$ cents on corn; in November the average was $25\frac{66}{100}$ cents on wheat, and $23\frac{56}{100}$ cents on corn—the difference being about 225 per cent. from the lowest to the highest average for the months of July and November, or 125 *per cent. less fluctuation on the canal than on the lake for the same time.* The total averages for each year have been very even. The average for 1861 from Chicago to Buffalo, was $11\frac{53}{100}$ cents on wheat, and $10\frac{56}{100}$ cents on corn; and in 1862 the average was $1\frac{4}{100}$ cents less on wheat, and $\frac{66}{100}$ cents on corn; in 1863 the average was 3 cents less on wheat, and $3\frac{4}{100}$ less on corn; and in 1864 the average was $9\frac{58}{100}$ cents on wheat, and $8\frac{94}{100}$ cents on corn. While for the same time the prices averaged from Buffalo to New York —

In 1861, on wheat,	...........15 75-100		On corn,	...........14 43-100
In 1862, " "	...........15 84-100		On "	...........13 76-100
In 1863, " "	...........15 39-100		On "	...........13 39-100
In 1864, " "	...........18 78-100		On "	...........16 55-100

Showing a constant gradual reduction. Upon a gold basis 1864 was cheaper than ever before, the money being so depreciated in value that the net results were not near as great as in the other years. About the same averages are also shown via Oswego. Thus the route has nothing whatever to do with the fluctuations of prices, they being ruled entirely by the law of supply and demand. The decreasing prices proves that our lake and canal facilities are now far in advance of the demand during the season of navigation.

II.

The facts stated in my former paper, fortified as they were by figures, suggest the very natural query: "*Why* do we need another ship canal from Lake Erie into Lake Ontario?" The Welland canal might be closed to our shipping for a short time, and that is the only possible reason that can be urged as a "commercial necessity" for building another. But to suppose the Canadians would commit such a suicidal act, is paying a poor tribute to those far-seeing enterprising men who conceived and executed the work for the mutual accommodation of both countries — they relying mostly upon our shipping for their tolls. "Self-preservation is the first law of Nature," and Canadians appreciate the maxim to perfection. We can afford to let them try the experiment. But let us see how it would affect the West, supposing they were to close it entirely. We have shown that there will be an abundance of capacity during navigation for all the produce moving from the West to reach our commercial centre without using the Welland canal. Having enjoyed the full benefit of its use for many years, Oswego has been placed upon an even footing with Buffalo as an outlet for western produce, but aside from the local business and the local interest, it has been of little or no value. As a fair criterion, take the grain and flour shipments for 1863, from Chicago, Milwaukee and Toledo by lakes to both places, and the result shows that there were shipped via Buffalo, 1,615,429 bbls. flour, and 42,526,370 bushels of grain, and via Oswego, 10,840 bbls. flour, and 8,099,234 bushels of grain ; in other words, from *those three points* there were sent via Oswego *five-eights of one per cent. of flour and nineteen* per cent. of grain. The small amount of flour shipped to Oswego as compared with grain, leads us to inquire, Why this difference in proportion? Taken in connection with the kind and quality of grain received at Oswego it suggests a doubt as to the "commercial necessity" of the proposed canal to the whole community. Out of the 8,099,234 bushels of grain received from these three points, 6,351,378 bushels were wheat, only 1,703,606 bushels corn, and only 43,250 bushels of all other kinds of grain ; showing eighty per cent. of the whole to be wheat. Milwaukee and Toledo wheat, being the best for milling purposes, furnished seventy per cent. of the wheat from those three cities.

Now is it possible that shippers, having no other object in view than sending their grain to one common centre, for a common market, at equal rates, should select one particular quality of one particular kind of grain, to send it by one particular route to get into the same channel, to go to the same market to be sold to the same men, to realize the same price as if it went by another port to reach the same destination? Common sense teaches no such commercial law as that. Why then are the shipments from these particular points of this particular kind and quality of wheat made via Oswego, while nearly all the shipments of corn, oats, barley, rye and Chicago spring wheat are made via Buffalo? Oswego can proudly boast of having the finest flouring mills, and manufactures the most if not the best flour of any city in the world. These mills require and do get the very best quality of wheat to grind. It has one of the most extensive corn-starch manufactories in the country. It has fine warehouses, lake and canal vessels for transportation to and from their mills and factories; it is surrounded by a fine and beautiful country; its men of business are men of enterprise and shrewdness, and they deserve success. By their indomitable perseverance, they have so far succeeded as to bring to their aid the favorable action of the various Boards of Trade — secured the influence of the New York *Commercial and Shipping List*, the recognized commercial paper of this continent, against the interests of its own city and State — and secured the passage of a bill by one branch of the general government in favor of building a ship canal out of the general funds of the United States, to accommodate a city of a few thousand inhabitants, under the plea of "want of facilities," and the bugbear of "military necessity," when in reality it is only a local milling necessity.

With the facts and figures before us as to our past experience, when both points of transfer were on a par with each other as to rates and facilities, it appears that Oswego, as an outlet for the surplus productions of the West to reach our centre of commercial values — New York or Boston — is out of the way of the natural channel. It is the front door on the back side of the house. As an outlet for Canadian grain, flour, lumber and shingles to a market alongside of our own productions, and to get a *particular quality* of wheat from Toledo and Milwaukee for their mills and factories, it does very well; but when they have "ground their axe," commerce again seeks its natural channel at Syracuse, and goes the old route from there, to the same commercial centre, to find a market.

But it may be said that we want to get out into the ocean with larger vessels than can pass through the Welland canal. But how do these vessels expect to get into the ocean without going through the St. Lawrence canals? The same "military necessity" that would close the Welland canal would close the St. Lawrence canals, and we certainly cannot reach the ocean unless the Canadians have a mind to let us. The only hope left in case they refuse will be the "marine railway," take our ships on wheels, go overland, around short curves, over bridges, under canals, through tunnels, regardless of expense. If they run off the track, never mind that; they only weigh about 3,000 tons — pick up the pieces and go on just as if nothing had happened; the consciousness will remain of having done "*a big thing.*"

But let us return to reason and common sense. If the Canadians have completed ship canals from Lake Ontario to the ocean, of a capacity to change the course of our shipments away from our own commercial centre, and not only transfer our carrying trade but our commercial transactions from our own canals and our own people to themselves, and the only thing wanting is a larger canal from Lake Erie into Lake Ontario, — should we tax the American people to build this canal; anticipate their wants; make their St. Lawrence canals valuable; transfer our business from New York to Montreal or Quebec, and pay $6,000,000 for *that privilege?* I *guess* no Yankee will reckon those things worth paying for. Do the people of Kentucky, Tennessee, New York, Maryland, Pennsylvania, New Jersey, or any other State, want to contribute their money or influence to a scheme to benefit a few localities? Or shall we let the Canadians build it themselves, and when done, let traffic take its own course, upon its own merits, according to the laws of commercial necessity and of supply and demand?

When the alteration is made in the locks on the Erie canal, we shall have facilities enough for many years to come to move property via Buffalo and Oswego during the season of navigation; and we shall gain nothing by adding the Niagara ship canal, unless we can bag the winds, storms and frost, during the winter, when other canals and rivers freeze up; or unless we can contrive to have it run as a hot water canal, and get vessels to run to and from it in winter; or get Congress to pass a bill to protect it from such slight inconveniences.

III.

As a "political necessity" the proposed Niagara Falls canal differs but little from many others. Local points want local improvements. One wants a harbor, another a bridge, another river improvement, another lighthouses, and a thousand other wants. The advocates of each rack their brains for arguments to lift the responsibility of paying for them off their own shoulders on to those of the generous public, as a "national" or "military necessity." Politicians and interested parties join hands and mutually agree to help each other through. In this instance, the real facts are, that in case the reciprocity treaty is abrogated for a time, and the Canadians retaliate by closing the Welland canal, a few millers at Oswego and Ogdensburgh might be compelled to get a small quantity of wheat via Buffalo. Hence comes the cry of "want of facilities," "military necessity," and "nature's highway," that have been set up by certain interested parties in our own State; and the echo comes back from the West, with the addition of "extortion in charges and tolls." They want "two strings to their bow," therefore they join in and sound the alarm from one end of the country to the other, until Congress comes to their aid with a bill appropriating $6,000,000. By what right does Congress enter the State of New York to build a canal which would rob the State of the tolls upon the canals now in use and belonging to the State? By what right does it seek to transfer the business of the Erie canal to the St. Lawrence canals — entirely out of the United States — leaving us to tax ourselves to pay our State bonds given to construct our canals? Have the States, as States, lost all rights to protect their own internal improvements from such encroachments? If built and used entirely as a "military necessity," the government might have power to construct the canal around the Falls, but for purposes of commerce I deny, wholly and totally, the right of Congress to vote away our State property and give it over into the hands of strangers and neutrals, or to benefit exclusively a few persons along the shores of Lake Ontario.

The West need have no fears of being ruined by extortion, until it can use more than one-tenth of the transfer capacity of Buffalo. Combinations have been tried, not because there was so much to do, but because there was and is so little to do as compared with the power and facilities to do it. No long duration of unreasonable prices can be maintained when the supply so far exceeds the demand. Politicians generally assail a successful enterprize for a division of profits or a reduction of their earnings.

The Erie canal, as a State enterprize, has been a success; and the "direct route," via the St. Lawrence, is harped upon to get a reduction of tolls without even a care for the effects or results of their patriotic efforts to impoverish our State treasury, and compel the taxgatherer to take the amount of our earnings and hand it over to the producers of the West, after having already reduced the tolls eighty-eight per cent. for their benefit.

The remarks of our State Auditor on this point, cover the ground. He says:

"When, in 1817, New York engaged in the then gigantic enterprize of making a navigable water communication, connecting lake Erie with the Hudson river, she could find no one to help her, or wish her good luck. We persevered, we completed the original work, and opened the facilities for planting an empire at the West, all of which was then, in 1825, a wilderness. Nay, more, we in 1835 commenced the work of enlargement of the Erie canal to meet the growing wants of that empire we had so essentially aided in creating, and the hand and arm that we invigorated and strengthened are now turned upon us and strike us down.

In completing our works we borrowed money and incurred a debt which we now owe and must pay. Shall we tax ourselves to pay this debt, and make our canals a free highway, to benefit those who will not pay any of that tax or bear any of our burdens? We have never sought or attempted to levy and collect more tolls on our public works than would enable us from that source to keep them in repair and pay the interest and reimburse the principal, as it matures, of the debt contracted for their construction."

If this is true, is it reasonable to expect us to do more? If the West wants the canal made toll-free, let the general government pay the State for its outlay, increase the capacity of the locks, keep them in repair, and run them free of toll. New York will go with the West hand in hand and shout "amen" as loud as it can. We want free country, free men, and free canals as much as the West does. But when a canal is a local benefit, the general government, in justice to the general public, and to those States having no interest whatever in the work, and who therefore ought not to be called upon to contribute anything to their construction or support, should let that section shoulder its own load and carry it, as we have done, and not seek to load us down with rival lines that do not enrich them, but make us poor indeed.

We may in time require additional facilities beyond what the increased capacity of the locks contemplated may give us, but we cannot judge our increased wants correctly by the figures of 1861, '62, '63 and '64. The closing of the Mississippi in 1861, and the preparation for war on the part of the South, suspended shipments of the surplus productions down their legitimate and natural southern outlets, and turned into the northern channel all the trade that formerly went down the Ohio, Cumberland, Tennessee, Mississippi and Missouri rivers and their tributaries, as well as all that was usually sent South by railroad. The Baltimore & Ohio railroad was rendered unsafe for business. The government occupied the first place for the transportation of men and supplies, and took from our roads just as many cars and engines as they liked, besides occupying all the workshops where more could be built; thus leaving a limited amount of rolling stock on hand. Under all these disadvantages — when the entire surplus productions were thrown unexpectedly upon our canals and railroads for transportation — *we did not fail to meet the wants of the West as long as navigation was open.*

The *unnatural* increase of business was not such as will continue. Comparing the amount of wheat and flour shipped from Buffalo and Oswego for the four years of the war, and we find there were shipped from Buffalo, in 1861 and '62, of wheat and flour, 1,638,579 tons and in 1863 and '64 we find shipped only 1,154,380 tons, showing a decrease from Buffalo of 484,199 tons.

From Oswego in 1861 and '62, 553,916 tons, and for 1863 and '64, there was shipped only 344,670 tons, showing a decrease of 209,246 tons. Buffalo decreased about thirty per cent., Oswego about thirty-eight per cent. The total decrease of tonnage in 1864 from 1863, was 704,751 tons.

The rates of toll on the canals have been the same for the last three years, and look at the decrease of tolls received. In 1863 the receipts were $553,736 less than in 1862; and in 1864 were again decreased $661,225 less than in 1863 — making a decrease of tolls in two years of $1,204,961. Thus far the decrease for 1865 is more than double that of last year, and the receipts are estimated to be only about one-third of those of 1862.

IV.

The facts stated in my former articles, in reference to the present light business on the lakes and canal, prove conclusively that with the return of peace, shipments are resuming their old and natural channels; and this, taken in connection with the supply needed for consumption at the South, is leaving us more canal and railroad facilities than we can make use of at a profit, except during a few weeks in the fall of the year. Buffalo has no control over the winds, and when there is a continuous blow up the lake of several days in succession, followed by a change of wind, there is sent into our harbor, perhaps a hundred or more vessels, all within a few hours. A hundred or more elevators would be needed to discharge every cargo so that the vessels could leave the same day. Four or five hundred canal boats would hardly meet such a demand, and it is unreasonable to expect facilities for such extraordinary circumstances. It would be as reasonable to demand another canal built to provide for accidents on the present one. I assert, however, that Buffalo can do as well, if not better, than any other port under such circumstances.

The Niagara ship canal would be of little benefit to through shipments, in years when a foreign market is supplied from other sources, as has been the case for the last three years. The exports from the United States from the 1st of September, 1864, to the 12th of June, 1865, to Great Britain, were only 1,615,083 bushels of wheat, 225,520 bushels of corn, and 97,844 bbls. of flour, the percentage being only 5 of flour, 9½ of wheat, and 2 of corn on what it was in 1861 and ˙62 for the same period. Ocean freights have not stood in the way; wheat and corn have been taken in steamships from New York to Liverpool for *nothing*, and three cents has been an outside figure the most of the season; flour has been taken at 6d to 10d per barrel. These figures do not look favorable for a direct route via the St. Lawrence and the Atlantic ocean. If we had a ship canal given to us we could not have used it for that purpose. *New York is the seaport of this country for grain shipments.* At New York we meet the ships of the world and orders for grain, if any, and we there meet the sale for our own country and the balance of the world; while via the St. Lawrence we come out into open sea and meet icebergs and get a taste of salt water. We find no customers, no destination but Liverpool worth mentioning, and that market overstocked. These *facts* do not foreshadow the " immediate construction of the Niagara ship canal."

The constantly decreasing tolls and freight on the State canals; the constantly increasing capacity to meet the wants of the West, at the same time that the cost of operating and keeping them in repair is rapidly increasing; and our desire to increase the capacity of the locks to give a further capacity of 200,000,000 bushels, should be a token of friendship and love between the Empire State and her sister States of the Great Northwest. We will decrease the tolls just as fast as the *increased* business will warrant it being done. If the West had a thousand canals it could do no more, and be just to itself.

Mr. Benton says:

" If New York holds a local position advantageous to exterior trade and interior traffic, is this a crime for which she must or should be denounced and punished ? If by her own means and the wisdom and forecast of her statesmen she has improved those local advantages, not only to her own benefit, but for the welfare of her neighbors, should she be denounced as extortionate because she says to them 'use these facilities for traffic in common with all the world by paying a fair and reasonable compensation therefor ?' If combinations exist at Chicago, at Buffalo, and at other places inimical to traffic, in which the State has no part or lot, the tendencies of which are to drive trade from our canals, is it right, just and proper for the State to levy these burthens upon her people, as she must and will do when she abandons the tolls on her canals ? Any government that imposes burthens upon all its citizens to benefit individuals, must soon lose public confidence, and will richly deserve the contempt of the world. Our toll rates are not, and have not been, any higher than they were in 1857 on agricultural products, when the tolls were paid and were payable in gold and silver, or an equivalent. Does the West complain of this ? Has she felt this conduct on the part of New York to be wrong, oppressive and exorbitant taxation ? "

There should be no rivalry or jealousies between the East and the West, for when we look at the " City of the Straits," or the " Garden City of the West," or Milwaukee, St. Paul, or any other city, county or town upon the broad expanse of this fair and fertile Western World, we find the seed from which sprang western enterprise and shrewdness — which has ripened into power and unexampled greatness and prosperity — I say the seed was the " universal Yankee." New York and other New England States planted the germ of this great Western Empire, which soon spread its fame to the over-populated countries across the ocean, inducing hundreds of thousands to seek homes upon its broad prairies. Now, no nation on earth — no Eastern State, not even Canada — can strike a blow against the welfare of the West without sending the arrows of affliction directly into the hearts of their own offspring and family friends. Therefore the Eastern States and the whole world respond and rejoice in Western greatness and prosperity. We will open the doors wider and wider, for its increased productions, as fast as as it can reasonably demand it; but we ask the West, in return, not to slight its old and early friends, or go stumbling over difficulties through Canada, down the St. Lawrence, out of the Gulf, around Nova Scotia, and along its dangerous coast to get to Boston. In short, we ask the West not to bite its own nose off, to spite the New York State canals.

I have been thus particular and lengthy in regard to canal navigation, for the reason that if the Niagara Ship Canal is ever built, it must be a rival to our State canals, neither of which can be used in winter.

The accumulation of freight on our railroads during a few weeks in winter, when all our Northern canals, lakes and rivers are closed with ice, has been a cause of much complaint, and from this cause the demand from the West has been made for increased facilities. Consider the circumstances in which our great Northern lines of railroad have been placed for the last four years of war. The government has taken all the cars and engines it pleased, and used all the workshops when more were to be made. It has occupied the lines for public business. After the government came live stock, next ahead of ordinary freight. Storms and intense cold weather set in, disabling the cars, engines and track. The scarcity of labor left the wood uncut, so that a supply of dry wood was not to be had. Iron was high and the passenger traffic was limited. The increased price of freight did not keep pace with the increased expenses.

Last winter was one of unusual length and severity. For weeks together the New York State roads could not run passenger trains on time. Some trains with six locomotives failed to make time, or get the mails over the road for days after they were due. At one time it took four days and nights to get the mails from Detroit to Buffalo. One storm succeeded another, until we had a total fall, during the winter, of ten feet and eight inches of snow. There were sixty locomotives disabled in as many days on one division of the road. The New York Central road, from the 1st of January to the 1st of March, only averaged from Buffalo and Suspension Bridge, over live stock, 280 tons per day; when in an ordinary time, with their full force, they can run a total of about 4,000 tons daily. When the snow went off, there was a flood, which swept away buildings, bridges, culverts and embankments into one common ruin, requiring weeks to repair the damages. Therefore, to measure the capacity of these railroads to move property under ordinary circum-

2

stances, by what was done last winter, is unfair and ungenerous towards them. There are now miles and miles of cars, rusting upon the track, waiting to do Western business at ruinously low rates.

The Grand Trunk road from Detroit to Portland, that threw the New Yorkers into spasms when it first opened, for fear of its taking all the business to Boston, being short of rolling stock, and having only an over-stock of floating debt to procure more with, did not come up to the mark and do all that was expected of it; yet it did carry a large amount of Liverpool freight from Cincinnati and Chicago at ridiculously low rates, to keep it away from New York or Boston. This was done to favor the line of steamers running to Portland, when the road could have earned from $40 to $70 per car more for the same freight to New York. It also favored bringing local Canadian produce to our markets, because it paid gold or Canada money to our lines, thus not only shutting out our own productions from our own markets, but largely swelling the volume of traffic on our own overburdened roads from our border ports to the East. The repeal of the Reciprocity Treaty will give our western produce dealers an increased capacity on our own roads, equal to that formerly used by Canadian property which was sold in our markets. Formerly our own shippers were shut out by it, and in many instances the Canadian shipper realized a good profit in our market, free of duty, while the losses were very heavy upon our own western shippers.

This combination of circumstances ran freights up very high, but the Niagara ship canal at that time would have furnished no relief whatever. The West could not use a $6,000,000 canal, with three feet of ice in it, to *cheapen* railroad freight while the winter lasted ; and in summer it could not use all our canal capacity. The government took from 1,200 to 1,500 canal boats and run them up the Potomac, the James and other rivers, and into the bays all along the coast, and they were never missed. With the increase in size of our locks as contemplated, so that a larger class of boats can pass in and out readily, New York can do all the summer and fall business of the West for many years to come. The "military necessity" is growing beautifully less every day. The overthrow of the late gigantic rebellion, and the complete success of our victorious army and navy, have demonstrated the power of this government ; so we should have no great fear of the Canadians "letting loose the dogs of war" upon us. Their ambition runs more to canals and railroads. They care more to relieve us of the heavy burdens of commerce we complain so much about. We do not desire to make war upon them. True, our own vagabonds have made some raids upon us from their shores, but no country is free from rogues and dishonorable men. Our own country furnishes a bloody illustration of this fact. Canada could no more prevent the St. Albans and Detroit raids than we could prevent men from going to Canada in 1837, and we know how hard we tried to prevent men from going there then! If our Canadian friends had done the same with us, and we had got no warning and friendly voice from their Governor General, our frontier cities and towns would now probably be in one mass of ruins. We do not charge them with cause for war, for that friendly act. They spent about a million of dollars in protecting their frontier — not from us, but to prevent our own people committing depredations upon us, and paid us back the money stolen at St. Albans by our own people. We certainly have no cause of complaint for all this.

We are not a nation of cowards to fear them, and they are far too sensible to invite war with us; but should that unfortunate time ever arrive, and that vast fleet of gunboats from England spring the trap upon the Oswego shipping, all "unbeknown to us," as feared by our Oswego friends, they will find our first "military necessity" will have been accomplished, and we shall (or should be) in full possession of their canal to keep them from using it against us. Our frontier would be north of their canal, and we should "fight it out on that line," using their canal for our "military necessity," instead of building another within range of their guns on this side of the river.

Therefore, as a "commercial necessity" we can do without the Niagara ship canal, and I deny wholly and totally the right of the general government to force it upon our State against its interests and its wishes. "Political necessity" should not so far forget the general interests of the people as to urge such a useless work at such a cost, merely to benefit a few persons, or to put business into the hands of others, or to furnish a particular kind of wheat to a few millers.

We like Oswego, we like its men and its flour, and we like its bread, but we think it wants a little too much government butter. The New York State canals cannot allow the West to take quite so much from them, merely to transfer it to the St. Lawrence canals, or to benefit a local few who are likely to disappoint themselves by trying to do all the business of the West, leaving Buffalo out in the wet.

RECIPROCITY

WITH THE BRITISH NORTH AMERICAN PROVINCES.

_____•_____

I.

Reciprocity, as generally understood in commercial transactions, means an equal exchange of commodities or productions, where each party is mutually benefited, neither having an undue advantage over the other. The notice having been given by our government to Great Britain to terminate the existing agreement between us and them as regards trade with the British North American Colonies, is producing a wonderful amount of argument from both sides of the line; and the most remarkable part of the argument from both parties is, that both have been cheated by its operations. The fact, however, that the inhabitants of the Provinces are, at heart, willing to continue the same cheat, although their arguments go to show that they confer a great favor upon us by doing so, must convince any reasonable mind that they have no faith in their own statements.

In order fully to understand both sides of the question it is necessary to understand in detail the working of the ordinary commercial transactions between the two countries, and the reasons why Canadian arguments do not prove what they appear to on the surface. Therefore, I purpose to take the arguments for the treaty, and reply to them as they appear to me to deserve, under the respective heads of Reciprocity in the Fisheries and Coal, Reciprocity in Breadstuffs, Reciprocity in Navigation, and Reciprocity in feeling between the parties.

RECIPROCITY IN THE FISHERIES.

"The speaker then showed the advantage gained by the United States in the fishing grounds and that when he gave his vote against it in the Nova Scotia Legislature, he said, 'What! Give up these rich fisheries in exchange for the worn-out ones on the Southern coast?' He said the United States had all the advantages.

* * * Now it was just such a proposition as this : Suppose two farmers lived opposite each other, and one cropped and cropped until he had taken the substance out of the land — no fertility left ; the other was just opening a virgin soil which had not been exhausted." — *Extract from the Report of Hon. Joseph Howe ; speech at the Detroit Convention.*

The " virgin soil " just opening, in 1851, employed as follows : New Brunswick, upwards of 500 fishing boats; Nova Scotia employed 812 vessels, 5,160 boats, 30,154 nets and seines and 9,927 fishermen ; Newfoundland employed 10,501 boats, vessels and fishing craft, and 46,857 men, producing 1,089,182 quintels codfish, 4,600 tierces salmon, 19,556 bbls. herring, 440,828 seal skins, and 2,636,800 gallons fish oils—valued in all at $4,455,484. In addition to these we have the fisheries of the Gulf of St. Lawrence. The above form but a portion of the fisheries, which were actively prosecuted three years before the treaty.

The entire population of the Provinces of Newfoundland, Nova Scotia, New Brunswick, and Prince Edward's Island, at that time, was only 664,051. Now it is quite evident that those few inhabitants did not *eat all those fish.* The United States, being their nearest and most natural market, had a population of nearly 30,000,000. If it was true that our fisheries were " worn out," where did we get our fish from ? Why, we got them from our colonial friends and neighbors, as a matter of course,—and on top of that we got from them 20 per cent. on every kind of fish, fish oils, &c., which the United States got as a compensation for the productions of their fisheries coming into our market to compete with our fisheries, which were not so much " worn out " as they would have us believe.

The returns show that the yield of mackerel and codfish, in Maine and Massachusetts alone, was $3,824,959, to say nothing about all the rest of our sea coast and our immense lake fisheries. Did we get Reciprocity by being allowed to send our fish to their markets, free of duty, when they were overstocked with fish and could pay us 25 and 30 per cent. duty and keep up such a vast army of fishermen before the reciprocity treaty ? They could bring their fish into our ports, and export them to foreign countries, without payment of duty. They entered at the port of Boston alone, in 1851, 92,312 bbls. of pickled fish, and re-exported to other countries 22,785 bbls., leaving 69,527 bbls. for home consumption, or for sale in our market that paid duty. At the same time the disputed fisheries were confined to the Bay of Fundy, and a few other points. Our people had the right to fish on the West coast of Newfoundland equally with the fishermen of England and France; and a joint right to fish with British subjects on the coast of Labrador and Magdalen Islands, together with the right to land at such places on those coasts as were then uninhabited, for the purpose of curing and drying fish. That right was of so little value to our men that they seldom availed themselves of it. We got the right to go into their waters and fish, and they got the right to come into ours, together with a market free of duty for their staple article of exports.

How near we came to having a war over these fisheries may be judged from the fact that the French are, and have been, fishing along side of us both ever since, and they do not fight. But few know that the French have Islands and fisheries there. The Colonies could not compete in the foreign market for the sale of their fish, owing to the bounties paid by the French Government to their own fishermen, amounting to about $2 per quintal. Therefore our market was the best and most acceptable. We paid a bounty also, and unless they could by some means get the duty off, they would fail to make fishing as profitable to them as they desired. Therefore it was an object for them to magnify the misunderstanding of our limits. We claimed to fish anywhere within three miles of their coast; while they claimed it to mean three miles outside of an imaginary line from one headland to another. Thus their interest was advanced by keeping up a war on the fishing question, until we were driven into making peace by opening our markets free for their entire business, for the privilege of having our fishermen pursue their calling without fear of being molested. How much we have gained by this concession may be seen by their own account. In the first prize essay on Reciprocity by Arthur Harvey, Esq., of the Finance Department at Quebec, we find the following statement:

"A return laid before the Canadian Parliament last year gives some important information on this score. It shows that the value of fish taken in our waters by American fishermen, which was but $280,000 per annum previously to 1855, rose at once to $632,400 in that year, and reached no less a figure than $1,265,700 in 1856. It then gradually declined to $416,000 in 1860. When the rebellion commenced, the war navy of the States needed and obtained the services of many fishing vessels and their crews, and the value of the fish taken fell to $250,000 annually.

So our fishermen only got, by their own showing, out of British waters, about $280,000 worth of fish in 1854; and we gave them over $1,000,000 in duties for the privilege of catching $280,000 worth of fish, which we had to sell at a very much reduced rate on account of coming into market with such an immense quantity of their fish. We thought we might make something out of it by going in on a larger scale, and in 1856 we made our big haul, and caught $1,265,700 worth, which was just about the amount of the duty we gave them for that year. Finding it an uphill trade, we "gradually fell off," and in 1860 were down to $416,000, and are now down to $250,000. What is the matter—have the fish disappeared? Let the same authority speak again and see. He says :

"If we now turn to the Eastward we shall see an entirely different scene. The Northeastern communities, living under a less genial sun, and possessing a less fertile soil, look to the sea for a great portion of their harvest. The value of the deep sea fisheries of Massachusetts, in 1860, was no less than $9,300,442 ; of Maine and Connecticut over $1,000,000 each, and that of the British Provinces $8,000,000."

Thus we have one State that has no less than $9,300,442 worth of fish, and the Provinces have increased to over $8,000,000. Our fisheries do very well for " worn out " ones, and it now becomes a matter of interest to know where the market is to be found for all these fish. Our war debt requires every branch of industry to pay its proportion. Our fishermen are taxed upon everything in connection with their business, and work probably as hard as our Provincial friends do. If we can furnish our own markets, we by right should have a fair chance of doing so. Why should our Provincial friends pay no duties or no tax, and yet have an equal chance in our markets with those that pay so largely to our internal revenue?

We are not disposed to be unfair, or to do our Provincial freinds any injustice ; but when they say " they gave us all the advantage," as Mr. Howe claims, and then in the same breath complain that our war deprived them of the market of " ten millions of people in the Southern States as a benefit to the Provinces," we have a right to suppose that the trade of the 20,000,000 of Northern people was worth something. Hear him :

" Again, when the civil war broke out, one-half the seaboard of the United States was blockaded, and all the advantages of the Reciprocity Treaty. so far as the consumption of the ten millions of people in the Southern States was a benefit to the Provinces, were withdrawn. Assuming that the treaty runs over ten years. it will be seen that for the whole of that period the people of this country have enjoyed all the benefits for which they stipulated, while the British Americans for one year of the ten, have derived no benefit at all, and for four entire years have lost the consumption of one-third of the people with whom, by the treaty, they were entitled to trade. Recognizing the political necessities of the period, British subjects have made no complaints of this exclusion, but it ought to be borne in mind, now that the whole subject is about to be revised."

We have " enjoyed all the benefits for which they stipulated," which by their own account, was to catch $250,000 worth of fish in their waters in return for a free market for their $8,000,000 worth; but our war shut out 10,000,000 of our people from buying from them! Recognizing the political necessities of the period, British subjects have made no complaints! This is certainly very kind.

Why not claim their right? Did we agree there should be no war? If we did—and there had been none—the price of fish would have been about $2½ per hundred. But there was a war—and while they modestly hint that they lost 10,000,000 of customers, they maintain a masterly silence about getting $10 per hundred for their fish in consequence of the war. This came out of the 20,000,000 of customers at the North, without saying anything whatever of the price got indirectly from the South, at Halifax, to run the blockade of the southern ports, without paying one cent to sustain the war on either side. At the same time thousands of our fishermen had "buckled on their armor," and were fighting to sustain the government, leaving our Provincial neighbors to enjoy the full benefit of our markets. "No complaints" under such circumstances! How magnanimous this was in view of the often repeated assertion for years, that the United States had "all the advantage" in the Reciprocity Treaty. Considering carefully the above facts in all their bearings, we must regard that assertion as "a fish story," having no foundation. Our friend Mr. Howe says the whole subject is about to be revised, when, judging from his arguments, he hopes they may get some advantages! We hope they will get justice and fair Reciprocity—no more—no less.

THE COAL TRADE.

Nova Scotia and New Brunswick have some of the best coal mines in the world, and from their proximity to Boston, Portland, and our other seaport towns, they can supply those markets, and pay a duty, cheaper than coal can be got from Pennsylvania or Ohio. In 1851 they paid 30 per cent. duty upon coal coming to our markets. The duty being taken off did not benefit the consumer, because these points were dependent upon them for supplies. With the 30 per cent. duty their coal mines yielded only 100,000 tons, while in 1863, they brought to the surface 429,351 tons, and in 1864 about 550,000 tons, nearly all of which came to our market and was sold duty free.

We have in Pennsylvania mines of coal which yielded in 1860, 11,869,574 tons of Anthracite, and 2,660,000 tons of Bituminous coal. This coal-interest now pays a heavy tax to the general government, while Nova Scotia coal competes with it in our market without payment of tax or duty. "But in return," say our Canadian friends, "we export from Ohio and Pennsylvania large quantities of coal to Canada, thus the Reciprocity is fair." Let us see. Canada has no coal of any kind, consequently the greater part of Upper Canada, being so far from Nova Scotia or New Brunswick, is dependent upon Ohio and Pennsylvania for supplies for general consumption, while we do not depend upon Canada for a market. Hence any duty charged upon our coal would not affect us at all, but would come out of the consumer. Therefore we do not care how much duty Canada puts upon our coal, so long as they pay it themselves, and it deducts nothing from our price. Before the reciprocity treaty the duty was only 2½ per cent on our coal going into Canada. This was to cheapen the coal to them, while we remit 30 per cent. on Novia Scotia coal and *pay it ourselves to them.*

Of this trade we got from Nova Scotia in 1863, about 300,000 tons, giving them about $210,000 duties. We sent to Canada in the same year 103,547 tons. They re-exported 82,206 tons, leaving only 21,341 tons for consumption in Canada, at the market value—no more—no less. We would have got the same price had the Canada duty been 20 per cent. instead of being free. That is another "advantage" which they gave us, for which they make no complaint, on account of the war.

THE WOOL TRADE—LIVE STOCK, &c.

Before the treaty we imported from the Provinces to the United States $100,000 worth of wool per annum. In 1863 the amount had risen to $974,000, all of which came in free of duty to be sold alongside of our Michigan, Ohio, and New York State wools ; our farmers paying heavy taxes upon their productions, Canadians paying nothing, but enjoying the best prices our market afforded.

We imported live animals worth,......................$2,390,799
And exported to the extent of.......................... 520,835

Giving the Provinces a balance on animals of.................$1,869,964

Which came here free of duty to compete with our own, the latter paying heavy taxes, while they paid none.

We took from them meats valued at.....................$ 256.527
And sent them meats the same year (1863).................. 1,238.923

Balance in our favor.....................$ 982,396

But the same remarks hold good in this case as with the coal. Our price is not governed by the duty put upon it in Canada, because we have a market without them, and even had there been a moderate duty in Canada, it would not have made any difference to us either in the price paid us, or the quantity sold them. They are consumers without a supply, hence must pay the cost—duty or no duty. These staples are not like the coal of Nova Scotia, sent to Boston consumers; while we have a supply, the freight from Nova Scotia to Boston upon theirs is so low that the producer can pay a duty and then compete. When the duty was removed, it went into the hands of the producer, which is not the case with the meats taken from us. They certainly did not buy it to the exclusion of their own productions, but because their timber districts required it for consumption, and their own supply was not equal to their wants. Therefore they had either to buy from us or not have it, and the fact of its being duty free cheapened it just so much to the consumer without adding one cent to our price. The duty on mess pork entering Canada before the treaty was only 12½ per cent.

II.

THE LUMBER INTEREST.

The lumbering interest is also a very important one to deal with in view of Reciprocity. That entire business comes directly in contact with our own people, engaged in the same trade, in a very different way from what it did in years before the war. Then both enjoyed the same rights and privileges in our markets. We gave the British Provinces 20 per cent. duty off their lumber, timber, shingles, wood, staves and shingle-bolts, for the privilege of sending our articles of the same kind into their market. That is, we were allowed to send our lumber, shingles, &c., away from a good market (which they were paying us a tax of 20 per cent. to reach) to their country that was already over-stocked; and if we sold at all, it would be at about 50 per cent. less than we could get in our own market.

This is another privilege we got when the Reciprocity Treaty gave the United States "all the advantage." In 1853, the year before the treaty, we received, from Canada alone, lumber valued at $2,383,184, Custom House valuation, which paid $576,636 80 into our Treasury, in order to compete with our lumber, which to a certain extent regulated the price. The Canadian manufacturers had to produce it for that much less, in Canada, to enable them to pay the duty, and as it came here and paid the duty before the treaty, and as our consumers paid no more for it than they did after it was made free by the treaty, it follows as a matter of course that the treaty admitting it free took just that much out of our Treasury, and put it into the hands of the Canadian manufacturers.

The average price per thousand feet of Canadian lumber, that paid duty in 1853, was $9; in 1854, $9 75; in 1855, when it paid no duty, $10 50; in 1856, $10 75; in 1857, $11 50; after which time the price again fell off to $7 75, and then worked gradually up again to an average of $10 in 1863. Thus it will be seen that before the treaty Canadian lumber cost us less than it did afterwards, proving that the producers in this case were the only persons benefited. We did not even increase the quantity received more than the natural increase of business. In 1853, the price was, on an average, $9 per M., and the total value received that year was $2,383,184, on which we received 20 per cent. duty. In 1861 the price averaged $9 50, and the total amount received from the same source was only $2,065,870. That paid no duty. The price was fifty cents per M. more than in 1853, yet the value was $317,314 less than when they paid the 20 per cent. Therefore we gained *nothing in price* and *nothing in quantity more than we would have got had the duty been continued.*

The conclusion must certainly be that our treasury is short just the amount of the duty. Taking the returns of exports from Canada alone to the United States, by their own showing, the value of lumber from 1854 to 1863 inclusive (ten years of free trade) was $31,528,513. The duty on this would have been $6,305,702 60, which went into their hands as another " slice " of " all the advantage." But when we come to take in the lumbering interest of New Brunswick, coming as it does into direct competition with our own in Maine, the value to them is very largely increased. Before the war, and during the continuation of the treaty, we lost only the duty ; but let us see how we now stand. Let us suppose two persons to be equally situated, the one on the Maine side of the river St. Croix, the other upon the New Brunswick side, both owning an equal amount of pine lands, and both contemplating building a mill to cut lumber for the Boston market. The Maine man pays a war-tax upon his land and timber ; he then pays a war-tax upon his axes, saws, chains, carts, cattle and horses ; his mill is made up of machinery, every particle of it paying a war-tax ; his transportation, sales and account-sales pay a direct war-tax; every paper and document have stamps attached, and if he has in the end made anything, his income tax must be added to all the rest. He brings his lumber into our own market, and gets no more than the New Brunswick man, who pays nothing, except the tax on his sales and the stamps on the papers required to transfer the property. Should we continue to admit lumber free from the Provinces, while the same class of industry within our own lines is so heavily taxed to meet our requirements, the effect would be to remove our lumbermen over the border, to depopulate our own lumber districts, and to enrich and build up the lumber interest beyond our lines. We cannot be just to ourselves, and continue to admit this interest to enjoy the full benefit of our markets without paying its proper share of the tax our own people pay for the same market. We must not discriminate against our own industry in favor of a foreign interest.

RECIPROCITY IN BREADSTUFFS.

In his Detroit speech, heretofore quoted from, Mr. Howe said:

" On the other hand, the Canadians seeing the great staples of the United States freely admitted into every part of the British empire, naturally claimed that their breadstuffs should pass with equal freedom into the United States."

This argument is used as a good reason for admitting Canadian breadstuffs into our market free of duty. Let us see how it bears upon our interests. Great Britain is and was over-populated, and did not produce a sufficient supply of food. Consequently she was an importer of breadstuffs; and any amount of duty which she collected from her own people was a direct tax upon their food, and increased the price to them just that much, without increasing or diminishing the price paid to other countries from whence they got their supplies.

The failure of the potatoe crop caused a famine in Ireland in 1847; but it was not a famine for want of food, for the warehouses in Liverpool were groaning under the enormous weight of provisions in store. The famine was for money or means to buy the food with. The famine produced such an excitement in prices that thousands upon thousands who could have purchased at ordinary prices were unable to buy enough to keep starvation from their doors. There was plenty of food, but those who starved, or suffered, had no money to buy it. The consequence was that hundreds of thousands of barrels of flour, sent from New York to Liverpool in the winter and spring of 1847, and which cost from $9 to $12 per barrel in New York, were piled up in Liverpool, and soured, and were sold in June and July, netting only 15 shillings per barrel, ruining thousands upon both sides of the Atlantic. Such circumstances, and close observation of the food question, proved the fact that a large proportion of their inhabitants were not able to buy dear food in an ordinary time ; and the failure of one single crop like the potatoe, brought squalid poverty, misery, disease and death to thousands upon thousands of their own people. Therefore anything having a tendency to cheapen food was a direct benefit to the people of Great Britain; and consequently their best way was to throw open their ports and admit breadstuffs at a mere nominal duty.

In doing this they did not single out the United States as the only country from which they would receive breadstuffs free ; but they opened the same privileges to the entire world, including Canada. We got no advantages over any other country. Our produce came into competition, in the Liverpool market, with the produce of the whole world. When that demand was supplied they wanted no more, and the law of demand and supply regulated the price, so that we got no more and no less than we would have got had they continued the duty upon all alike. They benefited their own people by reducing the price to them, while we were left in the same condition as before. On the other hand, the United States was a producing country. The surplus productions were counted by millions upon millions of bushels of breadstuffs seeking a market. Our centres of business—New York, Boston and other cities and towns—furnishing superior advantages for shipping, and sometimes a better market than other foreign points, rendered it desirable for Canadians to send a certain class of produce to our markets. At first it came in bond to be re-exported should a foreign market warrant it ; otherwise to pay duty if sold for consumption. This gave us the carrying trade, storage, commissions, etc., upon their business ; but it did not compel us to find a market in our own country for their breadstuffs in addition to our own surplus. If the navigation of the St. Lawrence was of such an untold advantage to us, why did they not use it themselves to get to Europe where the duty was free to them, instead of sending to our ports in bond ? Simply because they, like ourselves, wanted the choice of markets; and when they chose our market we got 20 per cent. duty in our treasury to assist in paying our expenses.

Let us see how we stood upon this class of trade in 1851, before the treaty, at only four points of entry from Canada:

	Buffalo.	Black Rock.	Oswego.	Whitehall.	Total.
Furs and skins, lbs.,	11,186	....	....	1,041	12,227
Lumber, feet,	10,200,427	12,393,957	74,209,425	24,090,425	120,893,897
Shingles, M.,	164,000	370	6,645	1,929	172,924
Wool, lbs.,	95,000	....	141,209	4,835	241,064
Flour, bbls.,	19,302	950	343.932	7,589	371,773
Wheat, bush.,	150,960	2,475	684,280	....	837,715
Oats, bush.,	12,296	....	111,291	243,084	366,671
Peas and Beans, bu.	....	....	64,896	21,132	86,028

If it was true that the Provinces only sent the above to our ports for re-exportation to foreign markets, and that their own St. Lawrence route is the best and only legitimate route for foreign business, then they certainly did not show much wisdom in sending it this way. But let us see how much they sent via Quebec, the same year. The total exports of Canada for 1851, were as follows:

To Great Britain (via St. Lawrence and United States in bond).$6,435,388
To the United States, ... 4,939.300
To British American Colonies, ... 1,060.544
To other countries, ... 826,688

$13,262,376

Let us separate the exports via Quebec, and see how much of the exports of breadstuffs went that way. The total export from Quebec in 1851 was $4,671,048. Deduct the value of deals, timber, masts, spars and staves, $3,796,084, and we find that the balance for all the other exports from Quebec was only $874,964.

This shows the natural result of the tendency of trade to the nearest and best market, even with a twenty per cent. duty hanging over it. Why, then, do the Canadians buy in our market a certain class of wheat, corn, and other grain? Because Montreal, Williamsburg, Cornwall, Maitland, and other points along the St. Lawrence river, have fine extensive flouring mills, without a supply of wheat to keep them running. The particular class of wheat raised in Upper Canada will bring a better price in our market than certain kinds of Western wheat. Canadian vessels, going to Milwaukee and Chicago with Canada lumber, can take our wheat back; these mills can grind it and send the flour suitable for our market back to us, and sell the balance for export or for home consumption. Secretary Chase's last report on foreign and domestic commerce, shows that

" All the exports of wheat and flour into Canada are from points west of Buffalo, and all the imports from there are at Buffalo and ports east of there on our frontier. The railroad lines terminating at Buffalo, Niagara Falls and Vermont, carry large quantities of flour, *much of it made in Canada from wheat of the United States imported from the upper lake ports,* * * * the trade, therefore, being one of convenience in transit, rather than one between producing and consuming markets, so far as wheat and flour are concerned."

Thus our grain supports their mills to some extent, and would, no doubt, continue to do so in case a moderate duty was placed upon wheat on both sides of the line; and while we should get some revenue out of their produce coming into our market, we should lose nothing on the price of ours, as the quantity sent there is not enough to change the market value at New York or Boston of that grade of wheat.

Our exports of corn, hides, tallow, etc., to Canada, are merely to fill a demand for which they do not provide themselves. The quantities of all these exports are small in proportion to the great amount raised here. We have a market of our own, and are not, therefore, dependent upon them for one. Consequently, it would make but little, if any, difference to us how much duty they put upon those articles, as it would come out of themselves, without lessening our sales or prices to any extent. Thus, while our people would be benefited by collecting a moderate revenue upon their breadstuffs, we should lose nothing by their paying their own government just as much duty on our breadstuffs as they think they can afford. But if the treaty raised the price of agricultural productions in Canada, it was because our market was generally better than their own; hence we could not have been much benefited by sending from a good market to a poor one.

Mr. Young, of Galt, C. W., says:

" The advantages of Reciprocity to this Province are so obvious that they need not be dwelt upon. As a country largely devoted to agriculture, a free and ready market was our great necessity, and that Reciprocity gave us. The immediate effect of the measure was to enhance the price of farm produce, of all kinds of stock, of dairy produce, wool, lumber, and many other articles of exportation. With improved prices, farm property, and to some extent other classes of real estate, became more valuable. In short, the prosperity of Canada during the past ten years has been largely dependent upon this enlightened measure."

If this is true (and who can doubt it?) we enhanced the price of farm produce, wool, lumber and many other articles of exportation. Why not give the balance of the truth and say just how much their productions were enhanced in value? *It was just the amount of the duty which we gave off, thus transferring the money from the treasury of the United States into the pockets of the Canadian farmers and producers.* New York being the centre of values for this continent, regulates the price of breadstuffs; and no matter who buys from the Canadians, or to what country it goes, the price is based upon the New York market, less the expense of placing it in that market. Our market being always overstocked with our own productions, it follows that by admitting Canadian produce free we contract to find a market for them in addition to our own surplus productions. Of course this advances the price of their productions, and decreases that of our own, while we get no advantage in the English market over any other country.

Russia, Prussia, France and Egypt can compete with us in their market, while none but the provinces are allowed to compete with our own productions in our market. The value of their entire productions is raised to the standard value of our own, whether it comes here, goes to any other country, or is used for home consumption. The price of every bushel of grain raised, sold, used, or even sown, is the same as our own; and the price of our own is reduced just in proportion as the total quantities of both countries combined produce a surplus dependent upon a foreign market for consumption. If the choice of markets was worth twenty per cent. before the treaty, it certainly is worth that now. We can hardly estimate the amount lost by us through the reduction of prices consequent upon Canadian competition in our markets. If we continue the same treaty, under present circumstances, we shall offer a premium to our farmers to leave this country and go to Canada to escape our war taxes, while we still give him the full benefit of our market. The same state of things would send foreign emigration into Canada, instead of the Far West. We cannot allow this and be just to ourselves. If, upon the contrary, the Canadian farmer were compelled to pay a duty upon his breadstuffs seeking a market in our country, and a tax upon goods purchased here, no matter from whence they came, Canada would soon be depopulated to our benefit. Canada could not continue prosperous under such a state of things. We cannot be just to ourselves and continue the Reciprocity treaty as it is. They cannot reduce the duty upon goods going into Canada from any country. Their public debts require additional revenue over the amount now collected. If they reduce the duty they would be driven to a direct tax to meet the current expenses of government and the interest on their bonds for public improvement.

THE BALANCE OF TRADE.

We are told that the balance of trade is in favor of the United States.

Mr. Young, of Galt, C. W., says:

" The transactions between Canada and the United States during the existence of the treaty may be thus balanced :

DUTIABLE GOODS.

Canada bought from the United States,..........$81,054,044
United States from Canada,..................... 6,312,819
   Excess of dutiable goods sold by United States,........... $74,741,225

FREE GOODS.

United States bought from Canada,............$143,114,010
Canada from United States,.................... 113,550,472
   Excess of free goods sold by Canada,.................... $29,563,538

           Balance against Canada in 9½ years, ... $45,177,687

This is one of the arguments used to show that we have " all the advantage." Without any further explanation it would seem fair and just. But let us dissect one year's business before the treaty, and see how that stands. Taking 1851, and they return as follows, viz: Dutiable goods imported into Canada from the United States, $7,971,380 ; Free Goods, $1,147,388 — making the total imports into Canada, $9,118,768. The exports from the United States for that year were $4,929,084, leaving an apparent balance in favor of the United States, of $4,189,684. But if we turn to page 427 of " Andrews' report," we find that the following are the countries imported from :

Great Britain, $7,358,988 ; United States, $1,081,372 ; British North American Colonies, $252,292 ; other countries, $484,512.

The merchants of Upper Canada, at that time, were either compelled to import their spring goods via the St. Lawrence, during the autumn of the preceding year, or else to get them in bond through the United States. When these goods arrive at the port of entry in Canada, they are entered as imported from the United States, when no one in the United States has ever seen a single article contained in the whole cargo. We have only carried the goods, while they were the productions of Great Britain. Of the entire amount of manufactured goods made in the United States, that we can sell to Canada to advantage, boots and shoes form one of the largest items. That trade, for 1851, was only $42,592.

The total amount of goods entering Canada from the United States from 1859 to 1863 inclusive (five years), as seen by Mr. Chase's report, on page 92, was $36,000,890; and in order to see how much of that trade belonged to the *United States*, turn to page 105 of the same report and it will be found :

For 1859, it was............................$4,185,516
" 1860, " " 3,548,114
" 1861, " " 3,501,642
" 1862, " " 2,596,930
" 1863, " " ....1,510,802—$15,343,004

Balance of *foreign trade through the United States,*.. $20,657,886

There seems to be some discrepancies in the accounts as seen by turning to page 103 of the same report. The "value of imports into Canada passing through the United States in bond," is given at $24,958,200 for the same period.

The Canadians, in their *official* returns of FREE GOODS, *entering Canada from the United States,* for 1861, '62 and '63 (see page 97), have an item of $8,045,184 of *specie and bullion.* The *export* of "specie and bullion" is generally to cover balances *against* the country exporting it.

But let us see another item of the way in which the balance of trade is in *our favor,* as they claim, and see how the *same articles compare in price* when *imported* into the United States from *them* and when exported *to them* (see page 89 for imports, and page 93 for exports) for 1863.

IMPORTS FROM THE PROVINCES.				EXPORTS TO THE PROVINCES.
Coal is entered at an average of, per ton, $2 68				At an average of $5 30
Dried Fish	"	" per 100 lbs.,	2 90	" " " 4 60
Fish oil	"	" per gal.,	58	" " " 89½
Wool	"	" per lb.,	39	" " " 46
Meats	"	" per 100 lbs.,	4 67	" " " 6 72
Flour	"	" per bbl.,	2 65	" " " 3 82

Our coal is estimated at *twice* the *price* of *theirs;* our fish at sixty per cent. *higher than theirs.* The grades of Canadian flour sent into *our* market are generally their *best* grades, usually competing with our best grades of white wheat flour, while what we send to Canada is of our *poorer* grades. Yet our POOR FLOUR stands upon record at FORTY-FIVE per cent. *higher value* than *their best grades.* This figuring shows that we "calculate" their *imports* are not worth so much as our *exports* of *the same articles.*' But while we are doing this they "calculate" the "balance of trade" in *our* favor *upon these differences in value put upon the same articles.* To make it more plain, we import from Nova Scotia 100lbs dry fish free of duty; they are entered at our custom-house in *Portland* at $2 90 cents; we send *the same bundle of fish on to Montreal,* which they enter there *free* of duty at $4 60; we have only transferred the *same bundle of fish,* and got a "balance of trade" in *our* favor of sixty per cent. of the original amount that the same bundle of fish was entered for at our custom-house in Portland, when perhaps that was all that we had to do with it, our *export* value being sixty per cent. more than the *import* value of the same article going from one province to another over their line of railway through our country. If we import at *gold* value and export at *currency* value, it is an easy way of getting figures to show a favorable result, when the facts may show a decided loss. Suppose they buy tea, coffee, sugar, dye stuffs, silks, laces, crape shawls, or any other goods of foreign growth or manufacture, in our markets, it contributes nothing whatever to the industry of this country. The merchant who sells may have made a profit; but they have not contributed a day's work, or one farthing beyond the sale and carrying of the goods to the Canada line.

But let us see what we got from them the same year. We find that they exported to the United States:

Ashes,	$ 65,992	Flour,	$1,181,484
Lumber,	766,628	Barley and Rye,	75,596
Shingles,	20,732	Beans and Peas,	41,588
Cattle.	140,176	Oats,	135,708
Horses,	185,848	Butter and Eggs,	76,012
Wool,	41,896	Unenumerated,	1,705,664
Wheat,	491,760		
Total,			$4,929,084

Thus, instead of having a large balance in our favor, we had from them the very articles that we raise and that give employment and strength to our country, mostly farm productions, and lumber valued at $4,929,084; while they had from us, as above, $1,081,372. Balance against us, $3,847,712; and when we deduct such articles as tea, coffee, dye stuffs, silks, laces, foreign goods, and sugar in bond, the above balance against us will be largely increased.

If we separate the other years' trade in the same manner we shall arrive at a similar result. We do not now have even the carrying trade to any extent, for the Grand Trunk Railway takes the largest proportion of it from Portland to Montreal, and from there through Canada; even the goods for the Hudson Bay Company go that way.

III.

RECIPROCITY IN NAVIGATION.

The origin of the Reciprocity Treaty is claimed by the Canadians to have been "the desire of the New England States for a settlement of the fishery dispute, of the Western States to obtain the right to navigate the St. Lawrence and the Canadian canals, the anxiety of Canada for free entrance for her natural products into American markets, and the advantages anticipated by many from closer commercial intercourse, at last brought about a change. The Reciprocity Treaty was the result."

The fishery question being disposed of in my former papers, we now come to the right to navigate the St. Lawrence and the Canadian canals, in which we got "all the advantage" again. We had the right to navigate the Welland and all the other Canadian canals before the treaty — that is, by paying tolls. Since the treaty we have, a part of the time, paid the full amount of tolls for merely passing through the Welland canal to Oswego, Kingston or Toronto, while Canadian vessels could pass into lake Michigan, run to our ports, and take cargoes of grain to Kingston or Toronto. The Canadians refund to their vessels ninety per cent. of their tolls, and while they enjoyed the full benefit of going to various ports on lake Michigan, to carry our productions, we could not take them to the same ports in American vessels without paying full toll. Reciprocity in that was ninety per cent. in favor of their vessels against our own. In the year 1850, four years before the treaty, American shipping paid forty per cent. more tolls to the Welland canal than their own shipping paid. They run through the canal 2,962 vessels, and we run only 1,799.

The free navigation of the St. Lawrence, to get out into the ocean, was the great prize we were grasping at. The "Great Northwest" were clamorous for that great "nature's highway" to foreign markets. We got that as a great favor in the Reciprocity Treaty, and I will now endeavor to ascertain how much we were benefited by it. If we turn to Secretary Chase's report, page 100, we will find that for seven years there was cleared at lake ports of the United States, to foreign countries other than Canada, 44 vessels, equal to 15,091 tons capacity, and that the entries for six years were 32 vessels of 11,261 tons. Let us examine into the great benefit of the grant to Americans to navigate the St. Lawrence.

The total tonnage in and out for seven years would not exceed two days' shipment from Buffalo eastward, and that little was not on American account, four of these entrances and clearances being Norwegian vessels. Nearly all the others were vessels belonging to and running as the "Cunningham, Shaw & Co.'s line," and even if they were registered as American, were owned in Liverpool and run entirely on Liverpool account. Patrick Tregent's vessels ran a few trips. One of these was the "John G. Deshler," which rescued the passengers from the wreck of the steamship North Britain. Mr. Tregent lives in Liverpool, and runs his vessels entirely on English account. So, instead of the Reciprocity Treaty being of any service to us, by granting the free navigation of the St. Lawrence, it has given Englishmen a chance to run English vessels into our own waters, and take freight from our own shipping, and carry it down the St. Lawrence for their own benefit.

Mr. Chase says:

"In the last fiscal year (1863) but a single vessel cleared and entered, an d it can, therefore, scarcely be necessary to make a distinct and precise account of it us of a permanent trade. This practical neglect of the St. Lawrence river as an outlet to western produce of the United States, under the circumstances controlling that route for the last four or five years, is particularly significant, and decisive as to the channels this trade prefers. Not only the treaty of Reciprocity, but the careful and inviting legislation of Canada in regard to tolls and tonnage duties, have united to remove all obstacles to the free employment of this route for the exports of breadstuffs and provisions from the Western States. Great hopes were entertained in Canada of the commerce that would be thus developed, *but the united efforts of the two governments have proved of little effect in opening a channel preferable to that made up of the lakes, the canals and railroads of the United States.*"

They made an extra effort, by the removal of the tolls, to induce western produce to go that way, and the Hon. W. P. Howland says of that effort:

"First among these circumstances may be stated the greatly increased production of cereals in the Western States. * * * That in proportion to that increase and to the whole volume of agricultural produce moved from lakes Erie and Michigan to tidewater, *we have not obtained so large a traffic, since the removal of the tolls, as we obtained prior to the adoption of that policy.*"

After enjoying the privilege of "giving something for nothing" for ten years, we are told, "If the expectations of the Americans have not been realized, they must have been unreasonable. It was not expected that this direct trade should at once assume colossal proportions." Let unreasonable Americans be patient and continue the Reciprocity Treaty. Suppose Canadian ships have had all the advantages in going into American waters and bringing away American produce; and supposing that the American people have been seven years doing two days' business via "the only reliable direct route" of which they have heard so much and realized so little — nature's highway is open to them yet, and Canadians are willing to be patient, and let others enjoy the same blessing a little while longer, provided they don't interfere with the other blessings which have been conferred upon them during the last ten years. Why throw away all the advantages when Canadians are willing that Americans should have them? Hope seldom told a more flattering tale than on this subject.

Let us ask some " unreasonable " questions, and tell some truths in regard to this great route which has been held up so attractively before us. If the St. Lawrence route is worth so much for our produce to get out to the ocean, why don't Canadians use it themselves, and take their produce to that free English market that they claim was made for our benefit, instead of sending over to Oswego and down our dirty canal to New York, paying tolls to us? The reasons are plain and unmistakable. They, like ourselves, want and must have a choice of markets on this continent; and that choice must be made in favor of *our American cities.* We all know that there are but few vessels engaged in trading up the St. Lawrence, and they are shut out by ice until too late for the spring trade; hence they come in ballast, to take timber and staves back, and do not look for much else. They arrive in fleets in order to be ready as soon as the ice will permit, to get their return cargoes. When they leave again there is no certainty of finding a vessel just suited for what is to be carried; there is an uncertainty and doubt about the business. During the summer months freight is not furnished in very large quantities. When it leaves Chicago for New York, it has the benefit of the Buffalo, Albany and Troy markets, and on arrival at New York has the benefit of the markets of the whole world, with ships ready to take it at once. Our fall shipments may go into store and be sold any time during the winter, while at Quebec, if they missed getting out in the fall, they would go into store for nearly seven months.

The straits of Belle Isle are closed with ice about seven months out of twelve, and are not safe during the summer months, owing to the strong current which sets through them, and the lack of harbors. The outlet via the Gulf, around Cape Race, is not much better. Those perpetual fogs which hang over the Banks, and hover near the southern and eastern portions of the coast of Newfoundland, are supposed to be caused by the tropical waters, which are swept onward by the Gulf Stream, and mingled with the icy waters carried down by the influence of the northerly and westerly winds from the Polar Seas. This meeting takes place on the Grand Bank. The difference in the temperature of the opposing currents, and in their accompanying atmosphere, produces both evaporation and condensation, and hence the continual fog. We remember the ill-fated steamer Arctic, which was run down by a French ship in a fog. We also remember the loss of eight or ten steamers out of one line; and we know, too, that we can only reach one market of any value to us by that route. For the last three or four years that has been

.worse than our own. Perhaps some of our Western friends expect to avoid Buffalo and Oswego and get to Boston and New York by that route. Let them try the experiment. From Buffalo to Boston via the river St. Lawrence and the Ocean, is 3,366 miles, and to New York 3,974 miles, against 495 miles from Buffalo to New York via canal and river.

We shall require something besides the free navigation of the St. Lawrence, which gives us the privilege of going 3,479 miles out of our way to get to New York. What merchant in Chicago is prepared to give an order for goods to come back on the same vessel which takes his grain over this route? Do we want to send from Buffalo to Liverpool, 3,213 miles, to find an uncertain market, or send 495 miles to find a certain market and meet the orders of the entire world? We think it will not require ten years more to demonstrate the utter worthlessness of that route to us as an outlet for our surplus productions. For those seeking a *pleasure trip* in summer, the scenery of the Thousand Islands and the Rapids of the St. Lawrence form one of the most delightful and picturesque trips in the world. The traveler that has not enjoyed this trip has lost a treat not to be found anywhere else in the world.

THE COASTING TRADE.

The Hon. Joseph Howe said in the Detroit Convention:

"A ship from Maine or Massachusetts, or from any State in the Union, may not only visit and unlade at the port to which she has been cleared, but she may go from port to port, and from Province to Province, until she has circumnavigated the globe, the discretion of her owners being the only limit to the extent of her transactions. The government of the United States gives to British subjects no participation in their coasting trade. Whether they find a market or not, they must break bulk and sell at any port they enter. With her fifty colonies spread over the face of the globe, your ship owners participate in the same privileges as our own. Your vessels are permitted to run to Halifax, from Halifax to St. John, from St. John to British Columbia, and from British Columbia to England, Scotland, or Ireland. They are allowed to go coasting round the British Empire until they rot. But you do not give us the privilege of coasting anywhere from one end of your Atlantic coast to the other. And thus it is that I say to my friend from Maine that in granting this privilege, with nothing in return, Great Britain gives you a pretty large slice."

Here is another pretty large slice with "nothing in return." We should be ashamed of ourselves and apologize to our friends for taking so much "for nothing;" but before doing so I would like to know when an Amercian vessel could load in Chicago and go to Toronto and discharge a part of her cargo, then go on to Kingston and discharge the balance without having cleared from Toronto to an American port, and then clearing from an American port for

Kingston again ; or why the steamers running from Ogdensburg to Montreal in connection with the American line must necessarily be British vessels, and why all passengers have to change boats, while a British steamer may be run from Toronto to Oswego, from Oswego to Kingston, Kingston to Clayton, Clayton to Brockville, Brockville to Ogsdensburgh, and from Ogdensburgh to Montreal, calling at every port, as soon as she gets into British waters ? If we load an American vessel at Chicago for Liverpool, we must not break bulk or discharge any part of that cargo at another British port. If we have any such right, my education has been neglected on that point. In 1860 the Canadian Legislature passed an act throwing open the harbor and district of Gaspé Basin, as a *free* port, without payment of duties. This also embraced an extended line of coast, with the islands of Anticosti and the Magdalen islands. The object was to furnish the small number of inhabitants on that large area of territory with the means of subsistence, and to induce others to go there. But no inducements have succeeded in doing much good, as that district is not capable of much development. They at the same time, opened the free port at Sault Ste Marie, embracing the whole Canadian coast of Lake Superior and Lake Huron, extending over 400 miles of lake coast, and the adjacent islands included. Under the same circumstances they can no doubt get permission to coast upon any of our *barren or desolate coasts as long as they like.*

A British owner of an American ship may load in Liverpool and go peddling all over our American lakes, into every town and city, and if he can get his vessel into the Mississippi, he may go on peddling British goods (if the duty is paid) to New Orleans and along the coast back to Halifax without any interruption. We can no doubt do the same in their waters under the same circumstances. Reciprocity in coasting is about an even thing.

RECIPROCITY IN FEELING.

Commercial intercourse generally produces a "reciprocity of feeling," and where those commercial transactions are materially advantageous to both parties, both are satisfied to continue to trade with and respect each other. The Provinces are, by their geographical position, material producers for this market to some extent. Our markets must of necessity be *their* markets for a large share of their surplus productions; but from the present necessities of both countries we cannot continue a system of free trade, unless we resort to measures more objectionable. We cannot be just to our own people and admit foreign productions free into our market, while we are compelled to tax the same class of industry in the case of our own people. Canada cannot reduce the duty upon our boots and shoes, manufactured cotton, satinets, machinery, shovels, spades, hoes, pianos, books and such other goods as we manufacture and want a market for, without reducing their customs revenue below their actual wants. On the other hand, if Canadians pay a duty upon their productions and upon all the goods, wares and merchandise consumed, it brings their net results down to so low an average that they cannot do justice to themselves and pay both ways out of their earnings.

To overcome these difficulties and continue our commercial relations, and do justice to both parties, will soon be the talk of statesmen from both sides of the line. They have some very clever, able, far-seeing men, and from our past ten years' experience, we have reasons for thinking they are quite as good, if not better, at a bargain than we are. If we should get some advantages for the next ten years, we will be no more than even on Reciprocity. Our necessities compel us to be firm and get such terms as shall at least put our own people on a par with them. We must not be exacting, and charge them with sympathy with the South during our terrible war. We are all liable to express a preference for a prosperous cause, although a bad one ; while we are quite as ready to repudiate any connection with the same cause when it fails. We may all be classed as friends of a paying cause, which we would scorn when it ceased to pay. While we must not harbor any ungenerous or hard feelings for supposed wrongs, or for sympathy with our " Southern brethren," we must not allow ourselves to be over-generous, and be flattered into terms by their profession of love and sympathy. I mention this, as we have been charged with enticing their young men away from their homes to fight our battles.

Mr. Howe said, in his speech at the Detroit Convention :

" We also have a charge against you. You have attracted our young men across the border to fight your battles. Where you can find one man in the Southern army from the British Provinces, you will find fifty in the Northern army. I, too, have suffered somewhat in this war. I have a son who has served in the Twenty-Third Ohio, and participated in many a heavy engagement. And when he showed to me the certificate of his commanding officers, that he had conducted himself with bravery and fidelity, it was some compensation for many anxious hours." (The audience here rose tumultuously, and gave three cheers.)

I have no doubt but that this young man did his duty nobly, and is an honor to his country and family. But our gratitude should be measured by the motive that brought him into our army. He has a most loyal feeling for the flag of *his* country, for Mr. Howe says : " Sir, the very boy I have spoken of would rather blow his brains out than haul down the honored flag of his country."

A noble sentiment, which should actuate every true American. But why did he leave his own country and take the chances of getting his "brains blown out " to sustain our flag ? If he entered our service when the first gun sounded to arms, and came into the ranks as a private at $13 per month, as thousands of our own brave and true men did, then I say we owe him a debt of gratitude which we can never fully repay. But if he waited, as many others did, until some thousand or more dollars were offered for substitutes, and with his money in one pocket and the other filled with letters from influential friends to our influential men, to get him an appointment as an officer over our own brave men who entered as privates, and was made an officer, and drew large pay from us for governing our men, then the gratitude should be from him to our government for his appointment, and to his God for sparing his life in battle.

The Provinces furnished about 40,000 names upon our muster rolls during the rebellion. Many perished in battle, some were honorably discharged after doing their duty creditably to themselves and nobly for us. It should be a pleasing duty to honor those brave men, and to sympathize with the friends of the fallen. There are some special cases which require mentioning in connection with this subject : Thirty-nine names appear upon our muster rolls as substitutes for drafted men, which I presume cost us about $39,000. Six months before the war closed only two were left to tell the story, and those two went before a magistrate at Clifton, in Canada, to settle their difficulties about the plunder, and there told their story. One swore he had enlisted twenty-six times, and the other thirteen times ; and out of the whole thirty-nine names on our muster rolls only *two* went into a fight. That fight was in Canada over the spoils ! Our sympathies are not very great towards those two, magnified into thirty-nine. Not one soul of them ever did duty in our army. They might have been two of our own scoundrels, seeking shelter in neutral Canada. From one family of highly respectable people in Canada are entered four names upon our muster rolls. Only one is now to be found, and he is doing duty for the State at Auburn, as a deserter—the other three being the same one magnified into four.

Thus, while we should harbor no ill feelings towards those who are our real friends in Canada—and I know we have thousands of them—we cannot forget that a few of the 40,000 names on our army list deserve more rope than gratitude at our hands. Our sympathies should not cover the whole number of names, without any regard to the motives and greenbacks that helped to make up that number. When our sympathies are wrought upon by the patriotic deeds of those 40,000 self-sacrificing *names* to get Reciprocity in *trade*, we must be allowed some "reciprocity in feeling" to doubt the full number entitled to credit on *trade* account, after being paid in full at the time. We cannot reciprocate the feeling that we got "all the advantages" out of them.

We should deal with the questions of trade in a fair, honorable way, that will benefit both sides. They claim that we have the balance of trade; if so, they cannot complain if both put on say 20 per cent. upon all the articles that are enumerated in the present Reciprocity treaty, leaving the fisheries, navigation and other matters to remain just as they are. The 20 per cent. would no doubt protect our industry and keep it moving forward, while it would be only about the proportion we pay for our necessities growing out of the war and the cost of collection. Our relations will continue just the same as at present, and if our trade is so evenly balanced, then the treasuries of both will be replenished. In going over the entire subject carefully we must arrive at the following conclusions, viz. :

I. The present treaty must close, and no new one can be formed that will not tax imports as much as our own people pay for enjoying the same markets for the same class of productions. Reciprocity will admit of our productions being taxed the same amount when sold in their market.

II. Our rights gained in the fisheries are a poor compensation for their fish, coal, gypsum, lumber, grind stones, granite and other commodities, entering our markets free of duty.

III. While we admit some advantages to some of our lumbermen in running the St. John's river in New Brunswick, we contend that we have enjoyed no benefit whatever from the free navigation of the St. Lawrence, for our shipping doing a through business to foreign ports. If there has been any benefit at all, it has accrued to British subjects entirely. Perhaps there have been twenty-five Americans who have been benefited by the Quebec market for staves and timber.

IV. We derived no benefit from the use of the Welland Canal that we did not have before the treaty, and that we paid for a part of the time with a discrimination of 90 per cent. against our own vessels.

V. We can see no equivalent for the free navigation by their vessels of Lake Michigan, which they can use and do our business from our own ports to our own ports on Lake Ontario, by clearing their vessels from Chicago to Port Colborne; consigning to some one at Port Dalhousie, and sending freights over the Welland Railroad, twenty-eight miles, another British vessel taking the same freight with bill of lading from there to Oswego. That is another "advantage" we do not get from them.

Finally: Our commercial relations must be continued, or "reciprocity in feeling" will decline. We desire a fair treaty, based upon principles of fact and justice to both parties, and I can see no better way *than to leave the present treaty in all its bearings, but agreeing upon a uniform tariff in both countries upon all articles mentioned in it as free goods;* or in case of the confederation of the British North American Colonies into *one* Government, then arrangements might be entered into between them and the Government of the United States to have *one uniform tariff upon all foreign goods,* and one system of *internal revenue,* so that neither party could smuggle goods to the other to any advantage. Then *abolish all Custom House Offices on both sides of our extended frontier, and have trade and navigation free and unobstructed* between the *United States and the Confederated Colonies of British North America.* The expenses of both countries would be materially reduced. Their *treasury would be replenished,* furnishing them the means to extend their public improvements,—and our *manufactured goods* would compete upon an equal footing with their own, *as an equivalent for their productions having the benefit of the markets of the United States, and secure to both that freedom of trade and navigation so essential for the mutual benefit and prosperity of both countries.* Thus while the two governments would be separate like our State Governments, *trade and commerce would know no difference between the two.* That is all the "annexation" they want with us at present, and we certainly have territory enough now, not to desire any more. *Uniform tariff on foreign imports, uniform system of internal revenue, uniform security of the rights of property, uniform system of weights and measures, with free trade and navigation, might cover all our difficulties and unite us as one people! bringing together in harmony and good feeling, the flags of two nations, the most enlightened and powerful on earth, into one interest, and that one interest would be mutual protection, and* "Peace and good will towards men."

RECIPROCITY.

SPEECH OF HON. ISRAEL T. HATCH, OF BUFFALO,

IN THE COMMERCIAL CONVENTION, JULY 14, 1865.

Reciprocal trade with the Canadas and other North American British Provinces has received the sanction of the leading statesmen of all former political parties in this country.

The territory of the Provinces is extended on a boundary indented with our own across the continent. Climate, soil and the cost of labor, the main elements of value in cereal productions, are nearly alike in both countries. These similitudes no doubt suggested the idea of reciprocal trade and commerce, and the discussion, legislation and diplomacy of the country finally gave it a practical application in the adoption of the so-called Reciprocity Treaty. The principle of the treaty itself was to permit the interchange of products between the countries free of duty; and equivalent benefits were expected to follow to each. It was a formal movement in substantial free trade. The belief entertained by an American Congress that its spirit and its substance had been disregarded by the leading British Provinces, no doubt led to its abrogation by the last Congress, and the refusal to authorize any negotiations for its renewal. The treaty expires in a few months under the notice given by the President for its termination, and our commercial intercourse with British Provinces, so far as the Reciprocity Treaty affected or changed it, is again open for discussion and legislation or diplomacy.

A brief reference to the history of our commercial relations with the North American British Provinces, and a review of the leading features of the statistics of trade with them for the last eight years, furnish the only safe guides to conclusions which should govern the action of this Convention. The examination will disclose grievances, if any exist, and mutual explanations, made in a fraternal spirit, may lead to the removal of the cause, and the restoration of those free commercial relations (so soon to terminate) upon a more enduring basis.

The commerce between the United States and the British Provinces, reviewed from the central point upon the chain of our most magnificent inland seas where this Convention now sits, now reveals to us the anomalous spectacle of two border nations with an array of custom-houses extending along their whole conterminous frontiers, sustained at an expense to this Government heretofore exceeding the revenue they collect, whose principal occupation is to enter and register the free products of Canada on their way to our free markets; while on the opposite shore, often separated from us only by a bridge, a ferry, or a boundary line, is found an equally extended cordon of imperial customs' buildings, collecting large revenues on our taxed products, as a tribute which the unfriendly legislation of Provincial Parliaments has exacted from us in exchange for the commercial freedom we have granted to the Canadas. These exactions have been justified on the ground that no special provision against them was inserted in the treaty, although its avowed object was to carry out the principle of Reciprocity, and " especially to regulate the commerce and navigation between Her Majesty's possessions in North America and the United States in such a manner as to render the same reciprocally beneficial and satisfactory."

Official Canadian reports show that in 1859 the amount of duties collected by the Canadas on imports from the United States was in in 1859, $1,825,135 ; in 1860, $1,759,928, and in 1861, $1,584,892.

During these three years the whole value of property imported into this country from the Canadas, upon which duty was levied, was only, in 1859, $434,532 ; in 1860, $358,240 ; and in 1861, $227,859. The average amount of duty annually levied and collected on these imports, in these three years, would probably not exceed $75,000.

The average annual value of property entering Canada, from the United States, in the eight years preceding 1863, upon which duties have been imposed, is $8,401,481, while Canadian goods entering the United States during the same period only paid duty on an annual average value of $467,238.

It will thus be seen that duty is paid on goods of the United States entering Canada to the average annual excess in value, over those of Canada entering this country, of $7,934,241.

The value of free goods imported into Canada from the United States, for the last eight years, has been $73,215,623. The export of free goods from the Canadas into the United States for the same period has been $115,548,880. The result has been the exoneration from duty of goods imported from Canada to the value of $42,333,257 more than the value of the goods imported from the United States into Canada in the eight years which have been referred to.

On closer examination it will be seen that a large proportion of the duty paying articles imported from Canada consist of commodities not produced in that country. In 1858, the dutiable importations from Canada were only $313,953, of which iron, hardware and salt (articles not produced in Canada for exportation, in any appreciable quantities) alone furnished $193,595. Of the remainder, a considerable portion was also of foreign origin. As the same reasoning applies also to other years, the following tabular statement for the term of four years, ending June 30, 1859, is added :

	1856.	1857.	1858.	1859.
Total amount of duty-paying articles imported into the U. S. from Canada, ...	$640,375	$691,097	$313,953	$504,969
Iron, hardware and salt, ...	503,995	531,011	193,595	349,555
Amount of Canadian and other goods charged with duties in the U. S.......	$136,380	$160,086	$120,358	$155,414

This statement demonstrates that during these years we have not collected annually duties on much more than $100,000 in value of merchandise actually produced in Canada ; which, contributing an average duty of 20 per cent. produces only $25,000 towards defraying the immense yearly expense incident to our custom-house system, along a frontier of inland coast 6,000 miles in extent.

The Canadian duties have been increased from time to time since the adoption of the Reciprocity Treaty ; and during the five years commencing in 1855 and ending in 1859, duties were exacted on the declared value of chief articles of consumption, as exhibited in the following table :

ARTICLES.	1855.	1856.	1857.	1858.	1859.		
Molasses, ...	16	11	11	18	30	per cent.	
Sugar, refined, ...	32	28	25	26½	40	"	"
Sugar, other	27½	20	17½	21	30	"	"
Boots and shoes, ...	12½	14½	20	21	25	"	"
Harness	12½	17	20	21	25	"	"
Cotton Goods	12½	13½	15	15	20	"	"
Iron Goods	12½	18½	15	16	20	"	"
Silk Goods, ...	12½	13½	15	17	20	"	"
Wool goods, ...	12½	14	15	18	20	"	"

Almost every year a new tariff has been enacted in Canada, each inflicting higher duties upon the chief productions of American labor.

The tariff of 1859 was avowedly based upon an exclusive policy. It was supported on this ground alike by ministerial organs of the press, by petitions in its favor, and by members of the Colonial Parliament. After securing our free market for all Canadian productions, its advocates argued that it was the interest of the Canadians to become independent of all other countries, and to employ their own ships and their own people; thus, to employ their own language, "keeping in the country all that is now paid to the United States."

No justification for the annual increase in these rates can be found in the assertion that the then present rates did not exceed our own. When the treaty was ratified, our tariff exceeded theirs, and the consideration given to them was not an equality of tariffs, but an interchange of the produce of both countries and certain privileges in navigation. A liberal policy towards our manufacturers was promised and had been before adopted; and thus the commerce and navigation of the two countries, it was expected, would be placed on " terms reciprocally beneficial and satisfactory." Justice to our people demanded that future Canadian legislation should conform to the letter and spirit of the treaty.

Certainly the spirit of the treaty has not been thus observed, and the increase of Canadian duties has not only affected our trade and commerce injuriously, but the manner in which they were levied has increased the burden, and now operates as a system of differential duties against us.

Canada now endeavors to deprive us of all the benefits of reciprocal trade by levying duties on the value of goods at the place of purchase. The people of Western Canada were accustomed to buy their wines, spirits, groceries, and East and West India produce, besides many other commodities, at New York, Boston or Montreal. The former system admitted American cities to competition —the duties having been specific and levied on the weight, measure, or number of articles wherever they were purchased. Thus no greater duty was charged on imports, via Boston or New York to Toronto or Hamilton, than via the St. Lawrence to Montreal. The present system forces the people of Canada to discontinue their business connections with our merchants, and buy from the Montreal and Quebec importer. Thus the productions of China, Brazil, or Cuba, if brought to Canada via the St. Lawrence, pay duty on their value in the country of their origin; but if purchased in our

Atlantic cities, must pay duty on that value increased by interest, freight over the ocean, and the various other expenses and charges of the insurer, shipper and merchant. This is not only legislation against our carriers, but against all our mercantile interests. The "increase of duty" has been carefully estimated to be 20 per cent. on goods imported into the United States and thence into Canada, in excess of the duties levied upon goods carried *via* Montreal. The distance from Cuba to Toronto, *via* the St. Lawrence, (a river closed half the year) is about three times as great as through the United States. Thus Canada vainly strives to conquer the laws of arithmetic, climate and geography.

The committee appointed by the Canadian Legislative Assembly in 1855, unhesitatingly affirm in their report (p. 3), "that the St. Lawrence canals were constructed at a large public expenditure, for the purpose of drawing the trade of the Western States to the ports of Montreal and Quebec."

The people of the United States are entitled under the treaty to use the river St. Lawrence and the canals in Canada, as the "means of communicating between the great lakes and the Atlantic ocean, subject only to the same tolls and other assessments as now are, or may hereafter be exacted of her Majesty's subjects." (See Article 4 of Treaty).

But as we are the chief carriers through the Welland canal of wheat, flour and corn—almost the only freight of our vessels by this route—a discrimination against us is made by imposing the same tolls on these articles on their passage through the canal, (a work 28 miles in length and forming the only means of communication for lake vessels between the upper and lower lakes), as if they passed through the Canadian canals. Yet we carry 25 tons on the Welland canal for every single ton we carry on the others. If the cargo is not delivered to an American port, but delivered to a Canadian port, the shipper upon the presentation of an official certificate of the latter fact to the custom-house officer at Port Colborne, receives a draw-back of 90 per cent. upon the tolls paid upon his cargo.

Exports of American goods to Canada show a marked decline during these eight years, falling from $6,790,333 in 1854, and $8,759,000 in 1855, to $1,560,397 in 1862, and $1,468,113 in 1863. It is thus demonstrated that the Canadian supply of foreign goods is no longer purchased in the importing cities of the United States, as before the treaty. The statistics of bonded goods entering Canada confirm this proof, and establish the fact that the

4

foreign supplies of the colonies are principally passed through Portland.

Although no duties avowedly discriminating are levied on American goods, the influence of the provincial tariff produces the same effect, for the manufactures most readily adopted by Canada must be like our own. The climate, price of materials, interest on money, wages of labor, and various causes, determining the kind and prices of manufactures on both sides of the frontier are nearly identical, when no legislation intervenes to arrest or alter the laws of trade.

If these views in relation to the injurious effects caused by the charges in levying duties upon our trade and commerce needed confirmation, it can be found in the arguments and expectations of the authors of those changes.

Mr. Galt, finance minister of Canada, in his report of March 1, 1860, at page 36, states as follows :

" By extending the *ad valorem* principle to all importations and thereby encouraging and developing the direct trade between Canada and all foreign countries by sea, and so far benefiting *the shipping interests of Great Britain*—an object which is partly obtained through the duties being taken upon the value in the market where last bought—the levy of specific duties for several years had completely diverted the trade of Canada in teas, sugars, etc., to the American markets, (our Atlantic cities), and had destroyed a very valuable trade which formerly existed from the St. Lawrence to the lower provinces and West Indies. It was believed that the competition of our canals and railroad systems, (via Portland), together with the improvements in the navigation of the Lower St. Lawrence, justified the belief that the supply of Canadian wants might be once more made by sea, and the benefits of this commerce obtained for our own merchants and forwarders. Under this conviction it was determined by the government to apply the principles of *ad valorem* duties."

At page 38 he adds :

" Any duty which has been placed on English goods is quite indemnified by the decreased costs at which our canals, railways, and steamships enable them now to be delivered throughout the province, and that if the question were one of competition with Canadian manufacturers the English exporter is quite as well off as before, while as compared with the American his position is greatly improved."

The history of the increase of taxation on American manufactures will disclose the fact—(as is asserted by the organs of the government) — that the increase was made necessary by Canadian expenditure in carrying out their system of internal improvements. That a large amount has been thus expended is shown by the following quotation from the Report of the Select Committee appointed in 1858, by the Legislative Assembly of Canada, to inquire into the course of trade between the different Atlantic ports in America and Great Britain, etc., (p. 3):

" The public debt of Canada has increased from year to year to about fifty millions of dollars, twenty-five millions of which have been created since 1853, principally in the construction of railways yielding no income." (See public accounts, 1857, p. 223).

Mr. Galt, in a report issued by him in England in support of a Canadian ministerial scheme, admits the insufficiency of the commerce of Canada to support her public works, and expressly states that, whilst possessing the most magnificent canals in the world, she is "without any trade to support them, except her own," and adding that the canals of Canada have failed to divert trade from the channels it had already formed; a system of railroads had also been constructed for the purpose of competing with American interests. (See report entitled "Canada, 1849 to 1859, by Hon. A. T. Galt, Finance Minister of Canada, 1860). He then proceeds to state that, after deducting a sinking fund for the redemption of the imperial guaranteed loan, the direct public debt of the Province amounts to £8,884,672, or $43,001,812 ; adding, that of this sum, debts incurred in consequence of the canals and other works connected with the navigation of the St. Lawrence, and railway advances, furnish £8,861,400, leaving only £22,272, or $107,796, as the total direct debt of Canada made for any other purposes.

These large Canadian expenditures in the construction of railroads and ship canals, were not made for their local traffic, as will be seen from ministerial statements, but to compete with our carrying systems in the transportation of property from the West to the seaboard.

To close these canals to our vessels would not only be an act of folly on the part of Canada, but would be contrary to the objects of their creation. The State of New York might with more wisdom close the Erie canal against the commerce of the Western States. That canal passes through the central portion of a State possessing much larger population than Canada, and from thence derives immense local traffic for its support, while the canals of Canada are lateral and depend almost entirely upon the commerce of the United States.

Of nearly all the articles named in the treaty a surplus is common to both countries; and we have an abundant supply and a surplus for export of every article named in it.

Canada has no crop so cheap and profitable for various manufacturing and other purposes as the corn bought from us, which was admitted free before the treaty. Wheat, the staple crop and chief export of Canada, was also admitted free before the treaty for the benefit of Canadian millers and shipowners.

For other grains, barley, rye, oats, animals, etc., we furnished for Canada the only market worthy of mention.

The Western States had from an early day looked upon the free navigation of the St. Lawrence as affording a natural and cheap outlet for their products; and believed that benefits arising from the concession of this national privilege, would more than counterbalance any incidental injuries to other interests.

Sir H. L. Bulwer, a former British Minister to this country, after pressing on our attention the spirit evinced by Canada towards our manufacturers, and promising on behalf of the Canadian Government to carry a liberal policy out still further, presented the free navigation of the St. Lawrence, with the adjoining canals, as the consideration to be paid by that Province for the free interchange of all natural productions with us, and for the navigation of Lake Michigan. The provisions of the Reciprocity Treaty were comprehensive, and included a satisfactory solution of the perplexities then existing in regard to all the commercial relations between this country and the Provinces.

Official reports from our foreign and domestic commerce gives us the number of clearances from Western ports to foreign ports for the last eight years, 44, and the number of entrances 32. In 1863 only one vessel cleared and entered, so that the concession of the free navigation of the St. Lawrence practically has proved not worthy of consideration. The co-operating efforts of the two governments have been unavailing in making it an outward channel to the ocean in preference to the canals, lakes and railroads of the United States.

To contrast the privileges, the United States had hoped to gain in exchange for the free navigation of Lake Michigan the free navigation of the St. Lawrence ; with the substantial advantages derived from our concession in this particular, it is only necessary to state the shipments from one port on Lake Michigan, Chicago, to Canadian ports in 1862.

The shipments from Chicago for 1862 to Canadian ports were : Flour, 420,544 barrels ; wheat, 3,098,424 bushels ; corn, 6,005,661 bushels ; oats, 187,252 bushels ; rye, 200,659 bushels ; barley, 71,919 bushels, reaching in estimated amount about one quarter of the total export of these commodities to Canada from Lake Michigan.

The aid of foreign and rival lines of transportation, entering within our territory, no doubt has cheapened freights, but it well may be questioned whether the loss to our carriers has inured to the advantage of the American producer. The value of the crop at home is actually established in its ultimate market, and the added supply derived from Canadian production must most materially decrease prices.

Our intercourse with Canada has been characterized upon our part by an amount of liberality and forbearance that is rarely exhibited by one neighboring nation to another.

It was enacted by Congress, March 3, 1817, that "no goods shall be imported from one port in the United States to another port of the United States, in a vessel belonging wholly or in part to a subject of a foreign power."

Whilst the United States has prohibited the transportation in foreign vessels from one American port to another, it has permitted Canadian railroads to transport property from one American port to another across their territory, although this mode of transportation is in manifest rivalry with the enterprise, labor and capital of our citizens.

All other means of transportation in the struggle to control the inland carrying trade of our country, are of minor character compared with the gigantic efforts of the Grand Trunk Railroad, owned by British capitalists. This road is one of the greatest works of modern enterprise. Few equal it in magnitude or importance. It reaches from an American port on the Atlantic ocean through subsidized American railroads, to the very centre of the grain growing regions in the valleys of our lakes and tributary rivers; and is to-day, and upon our soil, the most powerful competitor with all our various carrying systems for the supremacy over our inland commerce.

The recent movement in Great Britain to aid in widening and deepening the Canadian canals, for the passage of ships of the largest burden to our inland seas, and the revival of the project of an intercolonial railroad, cannot have escaped the attention of our people, and are deserving of the gravest consideration. In 1858, said Mr. Roebuck in Parliament:

"The present state of the North American continent was a matter of great interest to England. The southern and most important portion belonged to the United States of America, which ran up to where they met the dominion of England, which stretched from the Atlantic to the Pacific. England possessed the larger part of the continent, which proceeded northward until it reached, upon its western frontier. the territory belonging to Russia. We heretofore had planted colonies in the southern division that he had named. We had planted thirteen colonies in that country; those colonies had declared their independence, and had since increased to the number of thirty-five or thirty-six free States. We had created a power there which, if something were not done by England, as a counterpoise to the United States of America, it would overshadow not only England, but the earth. He believed that, in the Northern part of the Continent, we had the means of establishing the counterpoise which he sought."

"Taking the Western side of Lake Superior to the Rocky Mountains, they would cut the new colony which the Right Honorable Secretary for the Colonies proposed to establish, and he believed plans had been laid before the Right Honorable Baronet for carrying a railway completely across the Continent, so that a direct communication would be established between England and Vancouver's Island, by way of Halifax."

This was a magnificent scheme.

"The accomplishment of such a scheme would unite England with Vancouver's Island, with China, and they would be enabled widely to extend the civilization of England. When he referred to the civilization of England, he wished it to be compared with the civilization of America, and he would boldly assert that the civilization of England was greater than that of America."

The Colonial Secretary, Sir E. B. Lytton, in the same debate added, that this project would be "an essential arch, as it were, to that great viaduct by which we hope one day to connect the harbors of Vancouver with the Gulf of St. Lawrence." These ambitious views have, in late years, been expressed from time to time by British statesmen, and certainly are not referred to here to awaken any traditional prejudices, but to call attention to the fact that there is an attempt to give them a practical application upon this continent, recently shadowed forth in the negotiations of the British North American Provinces with Great Britain.

The past history of Great Britain leaves no room to doubt, as to the attempted consummation of any scheme for the extension of her imperial sway; for no power in the earth or on the earth, material, physical or elemental, has ever arrested the march of her empire around the globe. She seeks to grasp in the North the great commercial prize of the age: supremacy over the inland commerce of the North American continent. This gigantic rivalry is worthy of imperial ambition, for our artificial and water lines of transportation now almost extend into the centre of this continent, and soon must be connected by railroads with the Pacific. Over these transit lines are now passing the industrial and agricultural wealth of the West to the seaboard, and American and European emigration from the dense population of the East towards the Pacific. They lie, too, between these parallels of latitude in which the human race is ever moving in its exodus from the East to the West.

The extraordinary commercial struggle now going on between ourselves and our colonial neighbors, must end in colossal consolidation of American capital and enterprise, in some degree equalling theirs, or the field must be abandoned to a foreign rival.

The whole modern system of Canadian-British internal improvements originated in the freedom conceded to the trade and commerce between the two countries by the adoption of the Reciprocity Treaty. Without such concessions British capital never would have found investments in such immense works, nor could those works to-day find anything like adequate support, except upon the basis of our bonded system, and the liberal exercise of official authority under the act of 1799, and the warehousing act of 1854, (and certainly under the most liberal construction of the act of 1799), permitting the transit of foreign and domestic goods first through our territory, then through Canada, and afterwards to their ultimate destination in this country. The law of 1799 was enacted at a time when its framers could not have foreseen any such application of its authority as to permit the productions of American origin to be taken from one section of the United States through a foreign country, by foreign means, to another section of the United States, duty free.

No wise or even national policy permits such foreign rivalry. The argument seeking to sustain it would find its parallel in an attempt to defend the course which through the past years has driven our ships from the seas and surrendered into alien hands three-quarters of that foreign trade, once so much the object of our national pride.

The trade of the United States with other North American British Provinces than Canada, is upon more favorable terms, but in amount is of minor importance compared with the trade of the latter. Our exports to those other provinces are made up of wheat, flour, Indian corn, corn meal and rye. The fisheries of the coast provinces furnish a natural market for our provisions and breadstuffs, which can never be supplied so cheaply from Canada as the United States. Most of those articles, if not all, are necessities of provincial consumption, and many of them were admitted (as they were into Canada) free from duty before the adoption of the Reciprocity Treaty.

The imports of these smaller provinces to the United States, are mainly made up of coal, lumber and fish. The coal comes directly in competition in our market with the products of the coal mines of Pennsylvania and Maryland; and the lumber, with the lumber of Maine, Michigan and New York. The product of the mine must become, on both sides, a rapidly increasing class of our exchanges. Hitherto the balance has been much in our favor. Extensive regions, rich in mineral wealth, exist in Canada West; but her geological formations are destitute of coal, and, as the forests are cleared away, an incalculable amount of fuel from the limitless coal fields on the south side of lake Erie will be required in her northern climate. The coal of Ohio, Northern Virginia, and Pennsylvania, supplies advantageously the means of smelting the ores of Canada West. It will never be politic, nor will it scarcely be possible, for the government of Canada again to tax this indispensable necessary of life; and if the treaty expires, Canada would yet be compelled to buy it from us in increasing quantities. Its abundance in our territory. and its absence in the geological formations of Canada West, exhibit in the greatest degree, a natural adaptation to the system of reciprocal benefits.

The average annual value of imports from these provinces, paying duty for the eight years during the operation of the Reciprocity Treaty, was $216,172, while for the five years preceding, the average annual value paying duty was $1,751,000.

Upon the fishery question, New England authority must be regarded as most reliable. The Hon. Mr. Morrill, M. C., from one of the New England States, and among the ablest of her public men, says,

" To go back to the treaty of 1818, as the worst possibility that might happen, would subject American fishermen to the inconvenience of keeping off three marine miles from shores to which that treaty gives us no privileges, leading to occasional disputes, and might prove an injury to the mackarel fisheries; but these evils are not wholly insurmountable and by no means of the weight of the general considerations exacted of us as equivalents. These would be the proper subjects for treaties, and would be readjusted in some subsequent convention. It is no longer doubtful that our fishermen lose more by the free admission of fish from the provinces than they gain from the privilege of fishing inside of the line of three miles from certain shores. When the catch is short they make nothing, and when abundant the glut from provincial competition steps in between them and all legitimate profits. Besides, near-shore fishermen lose their hardiness and become idlers. Thus our people, renowned for their aptitude and success in securing ' the wealth of the seas,' behold their empire passing to the hands of strangers."

In presenting this summary of the results of commercial intercourse with the British North American Provinces, the exhibit of minor details has been omitted. The only object has been to bring before the people of neighboring countries, the precise state of our past and present commercial relations to each other and exhibit fairly, though briefly, the advantages and disadvantages resulting to each, under the treaty and laws which now govern their intercourse. The proximity and natural adaptation of the United States and the British North American Provinces to give and receive reciprocal benefits, easily and without humiliation conferred by neighbors on each other, have long been recognized by American and British statesmanship. Great Britain has expressed no official desire for the prolongation of the so-called Reciprocity Treaty.

The committee on commerce made a very elaborate report in our House of Representatives on the Reciprocity Treaty, (February 5, 1862,) wherein they argued that the grave faults already developed in the treaty should be remedied by a greater extension of the same system, even to the extent of the German Zollverein.

It would seem from the Canadian reply, that too much reciprocity was regarded as a " dangerous thing." Our offers were altogether too liberal, and Mr. Galt, in a report upon the action of the committee of our House of Representatives upon the Reciprocity Treaty, made to the Governor General in 1862, disposes of the proposition as follows:

" The undersigned can have no hesitation in stating to your Excellency that, in his opinion, the project of an American Zollverein, to which the British Provinces should become parties, is one wholly inconsistent with the maintenance of their connection with Great Britain, and also opposed on its own merits to the interest of the people of these Provinces."

Notwithstanding such objection to a freer, or too free an intercourse with us, a treaty no doubt might be made so comprehensive in all its details that neither party could be mistaken as to its results, or be capable of evading either its spirit or substance; or, our future intercourse might be left to reciprocal legislation, to be changed from time to time as the varying interests dependent on our international relations might demand, or the violation of reciprocal obligations by either party might require.

.